PURELY PUMPKIN

For Chloe and Ava.

PURELY PUMPKIN

**More Than 100 Wholesome Recipes to Share,
Savor, and Warm Your Kitchen**

Allison Day

CREATOR OF YUMMYBEET.COM

Skyhorse Publishing

Skyhorse Publishing books may be purchased in bulk at special discounts for sales promotion, corporate gifts, fund-raising, or educational purposes. Special editions can also be created to specifications. For details, contact the Special Sales Department, Skyhorse Publishing, 307 West 36th Street, 11th Floor, New York, NY 10018 or info@skyhorsepublishing.com.

Skyhorse® and Skyhorse Publishing® are registered trademarks of Skyhorse Publishing, Inc.®, a Delaware corporation.

Visit our website at www.skyhorsepublishing.com.

10 9 8 7 6 5 4 3 2 1

Library of Congress Cataloging-in-Publication Data is available on file.

Cover design by Laura Klynstra
Cover photo credit: Allison Day

Print ISBN: 978-1-5107-0965-2
Ebook ISBN: 978-1-5107-0971-3

Printed in China

CONTENTS

INTRODUCTION 1

HEIRLOOM PUMPKIN GUIDE 5

NUTRITION FACTS 13

BEVERAGES 15

BREAKFAST AND BRUNCH 51

SOUPS 85

SNACKS 99

SALADS AND SIDES 119

MAINS 153

DESSERTS 199

EXTRAS 239

ACKNOWLEDGMENTS 255

INDEX 257

CONVERSION CHARTS 271

INTRODUCTION

For living in the countryside most of my life, it's curious that I hadn't a clue before the age of nineteen that one could use pumpkin (or any squash, really) in desserts other than pie, and certainly not in savory cuisine besides mashed butternut squash with butter. Pumpkins were for carving jack-o'-lanterns at Halloween or table decoration, and they came from a can if they were to be baked into pie (though canned pumpkin does make an incredible pie). Pumpkin pie was my (and likely your) first run in with any sort of pumpkiny food. My mom's pumpkin pie recipe was illustrated (quite literally) on the bottom of an old ceramic pie plate, complete with darling graphics from a time before home computers. I still own the dish, using it exclusively for pumpkin pies.

Coincidentally, I grew up about five minutes down the road from miles upon miles of pumpkin patches. (I'd like to think this gives me at least some authority on writing an all-pumpkin cookbook!). These fields of humongous fireball freckles dotting the landscape are always waiting to be made into spooky art for your doorstep or edible art for your family and friends. To this day, pumpkin patches continue to instill a sense of cozy wonder in me, making me feel right at home—partly because they're quite near my family home, but also because they're the symbol of the season, generosity, and abundance of good food to come. (I headed back on a rainy fall day to photograph the spindly ground gourds—you can find the photos peppered throughout these pages.)

While my pastoral surroundings were idyllic for a woman who loves her vegetables, it didn't afford me the chance to try the omnipresent (and, I must admit, pretty tasty) pumpkin spice latté at my neighborhood—well, you know the place—as we didn't have one then, and the town still doesn't have one now. It wasn't until I ventured off to university that I, firstly, tried coffee of any sort, and secondly, tried a pumpkin-infused version. Over the last several years since my graduation, pumpkin and pumpkin spice (everything) has become a delectable

food trend in and of itself, and I'm here to celebrate and share its astonishing versatility with you.

The following recipes all use whole, real ingredients, much the same as I do on my food blog, *Yummy Beet*, and did in my first cookbook, *Whole Bowls*. Every ingredient I've used can be found at the supermarket or farmers' market, so no specialty food shopping is required; I've even given substitutions for any recipes using harder-to-find heirloom pumpkins. If you eat meat, any of the plant-based meals—though extremely satisfying on their own—can be enjoyed with your favorite protein. This cookbook is vegetable-focused, a term I inhabit in my everyday cooking life. The pumpkin's deliciousness knows no bounds!

From the creamy interior to the cozy pumpkin spice blend to the crunchy seeds and ludicrously green oil that's made from the seeds, pumpkin gives us plenty to work with—and I've employed it throughout these pages in myriad ways. Savory and sweet recipes, beginning with variations upon variations of homemade pumpkin spice lattés, smoothies, and breakfasts; followed by hearty soups, party-perfect snacks (or apps), salads and sides to brighten every fall and winter holiday—or everyday—table; main courses influenced by all corners of the planet; and, yes, a decked-out dessert chapter that will bring a bit of sparkle to your plates this season. You'll find classic pumpkin recipes (what's a pumpkin cookbook without the ultimate classic pumpkin pie, after all?), twists on classics, and an abundance of recipes that I hope turn into new classics for you during the fall and winter months.

All that's left for you to do now is tuck into these pumpkin-packed pages. Savor, share, and enjoy every comforting, moreish morsel by curling up on your couch, cooking away in your kitchen, or digging in at your table.

HEIRLOOM PUMPKIN GUIDE

Pumpkin is not a true vegetable due to its anatomy; it's a fruit, belonging to the Cucurbita family of plants that comes in a variety of different shapes, sizes, colors, textures, and tastes. The terms *pumpkin* and *squash* are often interchangeable, as they're both from the Cucurbita family.

Though not an exhaustive list, the following are the most easily sourced heirloom pumpkin (or squash) varietals:

American Tonda: Traditionally shaped with alternating vertical marbled green and yellow skin. Contrary to its name, this is an Italian varietal classified for having the "classic" American pumpkin silhouette. It's delectable roasted, puréed for soups or risotto, and added to salads.

Black Futsu: Intensely dark green skin with tiny bumps, a blush of yellow, and busy ribbing. The hearty flesh of this prized Japanese varietal is sweet with notes of hazelnut. Favored preparations include roasting and stuffing.

Blue Doll: A dusty, light turquoise exterior with several long pleats. With a shockingly orange, hearty flesh, it's ideal for savory cooking, from stewing to grilling.

Buttercup: Similar in appearance to kabocha with a slightly less vegetal taste and sweeter tasting flesh, buttercup is excellent sautéed, baked, mashed, or blended into soup.

Cinderella: Looks like Cinderella's pumpkin coach with its flat, round shape and traffic cone–orange exterior. Its flesh is custardy and smooth, making it wonderful roasted whole, stuffed, stewed, or blended into a silky soup.

Fairytale/Musquée de Provence: Beautiful, pronounced divots in its burnished, ochre skin. From the south of France, this large pumpkin is often found already sliced into wedges for cooking at French markets, though can be purchased whole.

Flat White Boer: Ivory-skinned, flat, and perfectly pleated. Its loud orange flesh is custardy and rich. This pumpkin is idyllic whole roasted or stuffed due to its show-stopping appearance and substantial texture.

Galeux d'Eysines: Decorated with "peanuts" on its peach exterior. The more "peanuts," the sweeter the flesh. This French varietal with supremely delicious meat is excellent for roasting, soups, desserts, stews, and more.

Heirloom Butternut: Similar silhouette to the more common butternut, but can showcase a rustier skin. Its deep orange, balanced flesh is ideal for purées, roasting, mashing, desserts, and more.

Hooligan: Very tiny with orange-speckled white skin. Slightly stringy and watery, but works well if hollowed and roasted for use as a soup "bowl."

Hubbard: Teardrop-shaped with a range of pigments, from dusty green to dark green to light orange. Delicious but hard to peel. Halve, seed, roast, and remove skin when cool to use in mashes, purées, soups, and desserts.

Jarrahdale: Soft green exterior and melon-like interior. From New Zealand, it's minimally stringy with a light, fruity flesh. It is lovely roasted whole, chunked and stewed in a curry, or sliced into wedges and steamed.

Kabocha: Squat with an intensely dark green exterior. This Japanese pumpkin has a dry flesh similar in texture to mashed potatoes. It is wonderful roasted, steamed, or turned into soup.

Long Island Cheese: Large and pastel orange (named for its cheese wheel-esque appearance) with a rich, hearty taste. I prefer this for decoration more than for cooking.

Marina di Chioggia: An Italian heirloom variety with an evergreen skin and deep orange interior. Its creamy, sturdy flesh was made for ravioli fillings, pasta sauces, gnocchi, and grilling.

One Too Many: Its name reflects its bloodshot eyeball, one-too-many-drinks-flush appearance. Not ideal for cooking but makes a fabulous decoration.

Pink Banana: Long, similar in shape to a spaghetti squash, though thinner and more pink in color. Its scrumptious flesh is not too stringy and is excellent for both savory and sweet dishes.

Porcelain Doll: Baby pink and big. Contains a deep orange, velvety, delicious flesh that can be used for roasting, stuffing, salads, and desserts.

Quaker Pie Pumpkin: Dusty-rose skin and classically round with an elegant, long vine. Developed by Quakers in New York and introduced to commercial markets in 1888. It's gently coconut-esque in taste, and while its flesh is highly edible, it's prized for its extraordinarily large flowers—naturally made for stuffed squash blossoms.

Red Kuri/Orange Hokkaido: Its tangerine, tear-shaped exterior matches its brightly hued interior. A Japanese, hubbard-style varietal. Creamy and sweet, yet slightly less saccharine than butternut and with a more complex flavor; lovely in both savory and sweet dishes.

Seminole: Looks like a butternut squash in both shape and color. First found growing wild in the Everglades. Its hearty, deep orange, dry flesh makes it good for roasting, mashing, and baking.

Strawberry Crown: Milky purple-gray skin kissed with pink on top and wide pleats. An idyllic eating variety with little to no stringiness makes this varietal suitable for any recipe, either savory or sweet.

Sugar/Pie: A classic pumpkin shape, weighing two to three pounds. Its name is a bit of a contradiction as it produces a stringy, watery, lackluster pie. Use this for

puréed soups and robust, savory flavored dishes. You can also clean and roast its seeds for an addictive snack.

Triamble/Shamrock: Murky, sea green exterior with the appearance of a shamrock (clover) from the top. Its agreeably smooth, fine-grained flesh can be enjoyed roasted in wedges, steamed, stewed, and puréed.

Turban/French Turban/Turk's Turban: Looks like it's wearing a hat with orange, green, and ivory markings. Its starchy, meaty, orange flesh is excellent roasted in cubes for side dishes and salads.

Yokohama: Its dusty, dark green exterior looks like lacinato kale. Native to Japan, its flesh is smooth and sweet with minimal stringiness.

NUTRITION FACTS

The pumpkin's health benefits are as varied as this kitchen chameleon's culinary uses. Its standout nutritional features encompass all parts—a food waste-reducing bonus as you can eat most of a whole pumpkin, top to tail.

PUMPKIN FLESH

Highly nutritious, the flesh of pumpkin and winter squash contains an impressive amount of beta-carotene (vitamin A), fiber, vitamin C, vitamin K, B vitamins, and several minerals. These nutrients contribute to skin, eye, and cardiovascular health, as well as sustained energy levels and blood sugar balance. It's a true "superfood," whether purchased fresh or canned.

PUMPKIN SEEDS

Pumpkin seeds (pepitas) are a source of healthy fats, fiber, protein, iron, zinc, and vitamin E, a potent antioxidant. Purchase pumpkin seeds raw and unsalted to minimize the chance of rancidity and keep sodium levels in check for use in recipes.

PUMPKIN SEED OIL

Pumpkin seed oil is rich in healthy fats including oleic acid, a monounsaturated omega-9 fatty acid. Purchase raw, unroasted to minimize the likelihood of the delicate fats oxidizing. Use for salad dressings, in smoothies, or as a finishing oil on savory dishes.

PUMPKIN SPICE

Your spice cupboard is home to numerous nutrients that support total body health, and the pumpkin spice blend in particular is packed with a few standouts. Containing ginger, cinnamon, black pepper, and more, the spice blend's antibacterial, anti-inflammatory, blood-sugar balancing, and antioxidant features will benefit you every time you add a sprinkle. To get the most nutritional bang for your buck—as well as ensure quality, potency, and big flavor—make your own blend using high-quality, individually purchased spices (see page **247**).

BEVERAGES

As I confessed in the introduction, I wasn't exposed to fall and winter's most pervasive, somewhat divisive coffee shop pumpkin spice latté until my early twenties. In the name of research, I knew I had to taste one so I could attempt to make it doable at home—hold the chemical taste, unpronounceable ingredients, and astonishingly high price tag. I grabbed a friend, ordered the famous brew, and took my first sip.

"Not bad," I thought.

But I knew I could make it my own. I could take this loved (and loathed) drink and transform it into a homemade version with variants. And, I wanted to make the homemade versions drinkable to the last drop—something I wasn't able to do with the overly saccharine coffee shop version (stalling one-third of the way through the latté was a little embarrassing). Though still a sweeter treat, my takes contain far less sugar than the original, while continuing to taste perfectly familiar and nursery-cozy. The sweet-heat and slightly peppery notes of pumpkin spice blend beautifully with not just coffee, but tea and chocolate, too. Find one you can't stop sipping and repeat throughout the season.

For the lattés, I'd like to give a special mention to Geoff Woodley of Detour Coffee (detourcoffee.com); he's a premium coffee roaster working to make sure that no one has to drink bad coffee again. They source some of the best—and my personal favorite—coffees and roast them fresh each week. Geoff assisted me with a little beverage research and generously provided the gorgeous drink styling and latté art on the Classic Pumpkin Spice Latté, Salted Caramel Pumpkin Spice Latté, Pumpkin Spice London Fog, and Matcha Pumpkin Spice Latté with Ginger and Orange Flower Water. Beyond pumpkin spice lattés, you'll find smoothies and an unbelievably healthy "pumpkin pie" smoothie bowl, pumpkin seed milk, and more. These pumpkin-spiked beverages are easy to warm up or cool down with. Pick your poison and start slurping.

RECITES

PUMPKIN SPICE LATTÉ BASICS
19

PUMPKIN SPICE LATTÉ BASE
23

CLASSIC PUMPKIN SPICE LATTÉ
24

PUMPKIN BUTTER PUMPKIN SPICE LATTÉ
27

SALTED CARAMEL PUMPKIN SPICE LATTÉ
28

PUMPKIN SPIKED LATTÉ WITH ORANGE PEEL
31

PUMPKIN SPICE HOT CHOCOLATE
32

PUMPKIN SPICE LONDON FOG
35

MATCHA PUMPKIN SPICE LATTÉ WITH GINGER AND ORANGE FLOWER WATER
36

GINGERBREAD PUMPKIN AND HAZELNUT SHAKE
39

PUMPKIN PIE SMOOTHIE BOWL
40

PUMPKIN PIE GREEN PROTEIN SMOOTHIE
43

VEGAN PUMPKIN EGGNOG
44

HONEYED PUMPKIN SPICE MASALA CHAI
47

PUMPKIN SEED "NUT" MILK
49

PUMPKIN SPICE LATTÉ BASICS

You can create many kinds of coffee shop-style lattés at home, and a high-end espresso machine with a glimmering milk-frothing wand is just one of them. (I wish I could say I have one of these; alas, I do not.) I've outlined a number of ways to get your caffeine fix, all producing slightly different but extremely delicious results.

HOW TO MAKE ESPRESSO

Coffee Machine: Brew a small pot of extremely strong coffee. Measure for use in recipe.

Coffee Shop: Go to your neighborhood coffee shop and buy a few shots of espresso. Measure for use in recipe.

Espresso Machine: Use according to manufacturer's instructions. Measure for use in recipe.

French Press: Increase strength by using more coffee and less water, adjusting until desired result is achieved. The following recipe makes medium-strong coffee (great on its own).

To a warmed French press, add 33 grams (1.17 ounces) coarsely ground coffee. Pour over 500 mL (2 cups) recently boiled water. Steep for 4–5 minutes, stir, and press. Measure for use in recipe.

Stovetop Percolator (Moka Pot): This is what I use. Use according to manufacturer's instructions. Measure for use in recipe.

HOW TO MAKE STEAMED MILK

Start with unsweetened plain nut or seed milk, unsweetened plain soymilk, or whole dairy milk. If using dairy, whole milk will taste best and create the smoothest foam; if you do go leaner, don't choose dairy milk with less than 2% milk fat or your latté will be watery, murky, and lacking flavor.

Blender: In a saucepan on the stove, heat at least 1 cup of milk until steaming hot. Add to a blender, secure lid, and cover steam vent with a thick layer of kitchen towels. Blend on high until frothy (about 1 minute if using a high-speed blender). Use in recipe as directed.

French Press: In a saucepan on the stove, heat at least 1 cup of milk until steaming hot for a single-serving press, and at least 2 to 3 cups of milk for larger presses. Add milk to press, secure lid, and quickly lift the wand up and down into the milk like a pump. Continue to pump until milk is frothy (1 to 2 minutes). Use in recipe as directed.

Electric Milk Frother (Steamer): This is what I use at home—specifically, the Secura Automatic Electric Milk Frother (500 mL). It creates pillows of steamy, frothed milk (even with non-dairy milks). Use according to manufacturer's instructions. Use in recipe as directed.

Espresso Machine Steam Wand: Use according to manufacturer's instructions. Use in recipe as directed.

Stovetop Whisk/Milk Frothing Wand/Immersion Blender: In a saucepan on the stove, heat quantity of milk called for in recipe until steaming hot. Tilt saucepan slightly and whisk milk to create a few bubbles (this method will not produce much foam, but it will warm the milk adequately), or froth with a handheld milk frothing wand or immersion blender. Use in recipe as directed.

PUMPKIN SPICE LATTÉ BASE

This base is the key to a spicy, warming, homemade pumpkin spice latté just like the coffee shops make—hold the hefty price tag, artificial flavors, and colors.

½ cup tightly packed demerara sugar (dark brown sugar)
½ cup water
½ cup pumpkin purée
2 tablespoons vanilla extract
1 tablespoon plus 1 teaspoon pumpkin spice (see page **247**)
¼ teaspoon salt

In a medium saucepan, warm water and sugar over medium heat until sugar is dissolved (about 2 minutes). Remove from heat and whisk in remaining ingredients. Strain through a fine mesh sieve into a glass jar. Seal jar and refrigerate for up to 1 month. Shake or stir before use.

CLASSIC PUMPKIN SPICE LATTÉ

The drink that started it all—and you can make it right in your own kitchen! Yes, homemade lattés will make a bit of a mess in your kitchen (and may be considered a labor of love), but there's no greater feeling than cozying up in your warmest sweater with a homemade latté in hand, slice of pumpkin pie on a plate (with a big, fat whipped cream cloud garnish), and good company on a chilly weekend afternoon.

Serves 1

2 ounces brewed espresso or brewed strong coffee (see page **19**)
2 tablespoons Pumpkin Spice Latté Base (see page **23**)
1 cup whole milk or milk of choice, steamed (see page **19**)
sweetened whipped cream, for serving (optional)
pumpkin spice, for serving (optional) (see page **247**)

In a warm mug, combine espresso and latté base. Top with steamed milk. Serve hot with whipped cream and a sprinkle of pumpkin spice, if using.

PUMPKIN BUTTER PUMPKIN SPICE LATTÉ

The pumpkin butter recipe in this cookbook gets quite the workout in my home (and in several of this book's recipes). Its caramel-like sweetness is much like the interior of pumpkin pie, playing off anything creamy. I love it with yogurt, ice cream, sharp cheddar, and much more. As pumpkin butter is quite viscous, your drink will be a touch thicker and creamier than the Classic Pumpkin Spice Latté (see page **24**).

Serves 1

2 ounces brewed espresso or brewed strong coffee (see page **19**)
2 tablespoons Pumpkin Butter (see page **248**)
2 teaspoons Pumpkin Spice Latté Base (see page **23**)
1 cup whole milk or milk of choice, steamed (see page **19**)
sweetened whipped cream, for serving (optional)
pumpkin spice, for serving (see page **247**)

In a warm mug, combine espresso, pumpkin butter, and latté base. Stir in a few tablespoons of steamed milk to thin. Top with remaining steamed milk. Serve hot with whipped cream and a sprinkle of pumpkin spice, if using.

SALTED CARAMEL PUMPKIN SPICE LATTÉ

Bust out your finest salt for this; I use a fine-grain sea salt in the base and a crunchy, flaky variety on top (Maldon) to provide textural contrast.

.... *Serves 1* ....

2 ounces brewed espresso or brewed strong coffee (see page **19**)
1 tablespoon high-quality jarred dulce de leche or thick caramel
1 tablespoon hot water
1 tablespoon pumpkin purée
½ teaspoon vanilla extract
¼ teaspoon pumpkin spice (see page **247**)
⅛ teaspoon fine-grain sea salt
1 cup whole milk or milk of choice, steamed (see page **19**)
sweetened or unsweetened whipped cream, for serving (optional)
flaky sea salt such as Maldon, for serving (optional)

In a warm mug, combine espresso, dulce de leche or caramel, water, pumpkin, vanilla, pumpkin spice, and fine-grain sea salt. Stir in a little steamed milk to thin. Top with remaining steamed milk. Serve hot with whipped cream and a sprinkle of flaky salt, if using.

PUMPKIN SPIKED LATTÉ WITH ORANGE PEEL

The afterhours pumpkin spice latté with a name I could not resist. This post-supper or après ski sipper tastes best shared with friends or someone special. Serve alongside a roaring fire—bearskin rug optional.

Serves 2

4 ounces brewed espresso or brewed strong coffee (see page **31**)
¼ cup Pumpkin Spice Latté Base (see page **23**)
2–3 tablespoons whisky or bourbon
2 cups whole milk or milk of choice, steamed (see page **19**)
2 large, flat strips orange peel (use a vegetable peeler), plus more to garnish
sweetened and/or spiked whipped cream, for serving (optional)

In warm mugs, combine espresso, latté base, and whisky or bourbon. Add orange peels to cups, spritzing to release the oils. Top with steamed milk. Serve hot with a dollop of whipped cream, if using, and an additional orange peel on top.

PUMPKIN SPICE HOT CHOCOLATE

It doesn't get much more festive than a mug of hot chocolate—the official tree-trimming beverage of the holiday season—until you add the spicy warmth of pumpkin spice. Save some for Santa, if you can resist.

Serves 4

¼ cup water

3 tablespoons cocoa powder, sifted

1½ teaspoons pumpkin spice (see page **247**)

3½ cups whole milk or milk of choice

6 ounces (about 1 cup) dark chocolate or chocolate chips, chopped

2–3 tablespoons light or demerara sugar (dark brown sugar), to taste

1 teaspoon vanilla extract

pinch of salt

sweetened whipped cream or marshmallows, for serving (optional)

In a medium saucepan, whisk water, cocoa, and pumpkin spice until nearly lump free. Add milk and heat over medium, whisking often, until very hot with a few bubbles coming to the surface. Slightly lower heat, whisk in chocolate and sugar, and continue to cook, whisking often, until chocolate is melted and mixture is smooth (2 to 4 minutes). Remove from heat and whisk in vanilla and salt. Pour into warm mugs and top with whipped cream or marshmallows, if using. Serve hot.

NOTES

This hot chocolate becomes a true holiday treat when accompanied by Spelt Pumpkin Spice Gingerbread Forest Animal Cookies (see page **227**).

If a thinner beverage is desired, add a touch of milk until it looks right to you.

PUMPKIN SPICE LONDON FOG

If you're looking for an alternative to the espresso-based sip, a tea steamer is just the thing. A London fog is a gorgeously fragrant, floral beverage made of brewed earl grey tea, vanilla, and steamed milk. For those who don't tolerate caffeine well, try antioxidant-rich, caffeine-free rooibos tea. Whether you choose caffeinated or herbal, I recommend starting with loose-leaf tea for the richest taste.

Serves 1

½ cup hot, strong-steeped earl grey tea*
2 tablespoons Pumpkin Spice Latté Base (see page **23**)
¼ teaspoon vanilla extract or paste or fresh vanilla bean seeds
½ cup whole milk or milk of choice, steamed (see page **19**)

*Steep this 2 to 3 minutes longer than usual—you want this strong, as the milk softens everything.

In a warm mug, combine tea, latté base, and vanilla. Top with steamed milk. Serve hot.

MATCHA PUMPKIN SPICE LATTÉ WITH GINGER AND ORANGE FLOWER WATER

Matcha's grassy hue and assertive taste pairs perfectly with gentle orange flower water, sweet-heat ginger, and warming pumpkin spice. Matcha can be found at some supermarkets, teashops, bulk food stores, and health food stores.

·· *Serves 2* ··

2 tablespoons Pumpkin Spice Latté Base (see page **23**)
1 tablespoon honey
1 tablespoon water
¼ teaspoon orange flower water
1 tablespoon matcha powder
¼ teaspoon ground dried ginger
1½ cups whole milk or milk of choice, steamed (see page **19**)

In a small bowl, whisk together latté base, honey, water, and orange flower water. Whisk in matcha and ginger until smooth. Stir in a little steamed milk to thin and divide between warm mugs. Top with remaining steamed milk. Serve hot.

GINGERBREAD PUMPKIN AND HAZELNUT SHAKE

This drink makes a fabulously festive addition to a holiday brunch. It's quite substantial, so I recommend smaller portions instead of one large smoothie. If you're feeling healthy and/ or inspired by the Halloween season, a handful of spinach is a tasteless and colorful nutrition BOO-ster.

For a thicker smoothie, add additional ice; for a thinner smoothie, add additional milk or water.

.... *Serves 2–3* ....

⅔ cup canned coconut milk or plain yogurt, chilled
½ cup–1 cup milk of choice (start with ½ cup, thin with additional), chilled
½ cup pumpkin purée, chilled
⅓ cup roasted hazelnuts, plus more to garnish
2 tablespoons maple syrup
1 teaspoon molasses, plus more to garnish
1 teaspoon vanilla extract
1 teaspoon ground dried ginger
1 teaspoon pumpkin spice (see page **247**)
pinch of salt
4 ice cubes

Add all smoothie ingredients to a blender in the order listed. Blend on high until smooth and creamy. Thin with additional milk or water, if desired. Serve immediately with a drizzle of molasses and a hazelnut on top.

PUMPKIN PIE SMOOTHIE BOWL

This gorgeous, trendy morning meal in a bowl tastes like the warming custardy interior of pumpkin pie and is sturdy enough to eat with a spoon (though can be thinned out for those who want to sip instead of spoon). Decorate to your taste with fresh or dried fruit, rolled oats, seeds, dark chocolate chips, additional yogurt, and/or nut butter. The more you sprinkle on top, the more substantial—and beautiful—this becomes.

For a thicker smoothie, add additional ice; for a thinner smoothie (to drink instead of eat with a spoon), add additional milk or water.

Serves 1

⅓ cup milk of choice or water, chilled
½ cup pumpkin purée, chilled
⅓ cup plain yogurt (Greek or Balkan-style)
1 tablespoon maple syrup
½ teaspoon pumpkin spice (see page **247**)
½ teaspoon vanilla extract
½ banana, peeled, cut into pieces, and frozen (fresh also works but makes a thinner smoothie)
2 ice cubes
toppings, for serving (pomegranate arils, pumpkin seeds, oats, banana slices, etc.)

Add all smoothie ingredients except toppings to a blender in the order listed. Blend on high until smooth and creamy. Pour into a bowl and adorn with desired toppings. Serve immediately.

NOTES

Smoothie portion (without toppings) can be made up to 1 day in advance.

PUMPKIN PIE GREEN PROTEIN SMOOTHIE

For when you need something lighter and packed with nutrition during the time of plenty, I recommend a glass of this verdant brew. A variation on the Pumpkin Pie Smoothie Bowl (see page **40**), you could even serve this to kids (or adults, for the young at heart) on Halloween morning and call it "slime" or "witches brew," if you fancy. As with most smoothies, substitutions are fine—smoothies are not an exact science. Nevertheless, I wouldn't recommend using kale in lieu of spinach as it's far too loud; spinach is quiet, allowing the pumpkin pie–esque flavors to come forward.

For a thicker smoothie, add additional ice; for a thinner smoothie, add additional milk or water.

Serves 1

⅓ cup milk of choice or water, plus more to thin, chilled

⅓ cup pumpkin purée, chilled

⅓ cup plain yogurt

1 tablespoon maple syrup

½ teaspoon pumpkin spice (see page **247**)

½ teaspoon vanilla extract

1 cup packed spinach

½ banana, peeled, cut into pieces, and frozen (fresh also works but makes a thinner smoothie)

1–2 tablespoons boosters (protein powder, flaxseed oil, peanut butter, pumpkin seeds, etc.) (optional)

2 ice cubes

Add all smoothie ingredients to a blender in the order listed. Blend on high until smooth and creamy. Thin with additional milk or water, if desired. Serve immediately.

VEGAN PUMPKIN EGGNOG

Vegan eggnog is a bit of a lie, as there are absolutely no eggs in here whatsoever. Replacing the eponymous ingredient are raw cashews that have soaked in water overnight, and have been transformed into a silky beverage through a quick whir in the blender. Just a hint of pumpkin purée adds body and sweetness and gives the eggnog its classic buttercup-yellow appearance. It's not required, but you can spike your 'nog if you're feeling extra festive. Nutmeg, however, is required for a true taste of this steadfast holiday beverage.

Serves 4–6

1 cup raw, unsalted whole cashews
8 cups water, divided
½ cup pumpkin purée
¼ cup maple syrup
1 teaspoon vanilla extract or paste or fresh vanilla bean seeds
½ teaspoon ground nutmeg, plus more for serving

In a large bowl, soak cashews overnight at room temperature (or for at least 12 hours) in 4 cups of water. Drain and rinse. Add soaked cashews to a high-speed blender along with 4 cups of fresh water and remaining ingredients. Blend on high until smooth and creamy. Pour into a large pitcher, cover, and refrigerate until chilled (about 3 hours). Gently stir, pour into glasses, and serve with a sprinkling of nutmeg.

HONEYED PUMPKIN SPICE MASALA CHAI

Pumpkin spice comes with its own built-in chai flavor, making one of my most-loved fall and winter beverages simple to whip up on the stovetop with just a few additional ingredients.

Serves 1

1 cup whole milk or milk of choice
½ cup water
2–3 teaspoons honey, to taste
½ teaspoon pumpkin spice (see page **247**)
½ teaspoon vanilla extract
¼ teaspoon ground cardamom
1 (½-inch) chunk fresh ginger, peeled
1 teaspoon loose-leaf black tea

In a small saucepan, whisk together all ingredients except tea. Heat over medium, whisking often, for 3 to 5 minutes, until hot. Whisk in tea and steep for 30 seconds to 1 minute. Carefully strain through a fine mesh sieve or tea strainer into a warm mug; discard solids (ginger and tea leaves). Serve hot.

PUMPKIN SEED "NUT" MILK

Along with being a beautiful pastel green, pumpkin seed milk is dairy-free, nut-free, and vegan, as well as high in minerals and healthy fats. Splash on cereal or warm oatmeal, enjoy by the glassful, employ in baking, or use for smoothies and lattés. Because this milk doesn't have any stabilizers or preservatives, a gentle shake before pouring is recommended to homogenize. Use within 4 to 5 days.

Makes approximately 3 cups

1 cup raw, unsalted green pumpkin seeds
7 cups water, divided
3 medjool dates, pitted, or 3 tablespoons maple syrup
½ teaspoon vanilla extract
⅛ teaspoon salt

In a large bowl, soak pumpkin seeds at room temperature for 2 to 3 hours in 4 cups of water. Drain and rinse. Add soaked seeds to a high-speed blender along with 3 cups of fresh water and remaining ingredients. Blend on high until smooth and creamy. Over a large bowl (one with a pouring spout is handy), pour blended milk through a nut milk bag or clean cloth and squeeze until pumpkin seed pulp is as dry as possible (see *Notes*). Pour strained milk into an airtight glass jar and refrigerate until chilled (about 3 hours). Gently shake before serving.

NOTES

Use leftover pumpkin seed pulp in smoothies, muffins, pasta sauces, salsas, soups, crackers, cakes, or granola for a hit of protein and fiber.

BREAKFAST AND BRUNCH

It's so easy to notice the sudden change in light that happens during the fall and winter months in the early morning hours. Darkness sticks around a bit longer, days grow shorter, and we all want a little warm sunshine to kiss our cheeks. Alas, our sunshiney hours are drastically reduced, condensed into a few golden moments that, depending on what time you leave for work, can leave you eating breakfast in the dark. Well, if we can't have that big ol' fireball in the sky greeting us when we hop (or crawl) out of bed, we can certainly try for it in our bowls and on our plates at that time.

Pumpkin's ability to merge into either sweet or savory dishes makes it a star breakfast candidate. Full of both healthy starts and heartier beginnings, this chapter is dedicated to those of us (including me) who absolutely require something of substance before noon. And, of course, the breakfast for dinner club, which I'm a proud member of, has not been forgotten, with dishes like shakshuka to spice up even the coldest evening.

Sweet or savory, eggs or yogurt, grains or greens, fruit or vegetables, scones or muffins, I'm certain you'll find something that makes your blaring alarm clock sound like angelic harps each and every morning this season.

RECITES

SPICED PUMPKIN OATMEAL WITH
BAKED PEARS AND PECANS

55

SAVORY HERBED PUMPKIN
OATMEAL WITH SOFT-BOILED
EGGS AND PUMPKIN SEED PESTO

56

PUMPKIN PIE GRANOLA WITH
PECANS

59

SUPER-SEED PUMPKIN SPICE
AND APPLE MUESLI

60

SHAKSHUKA WITH PUMPKIN AND
PEPPERS

63

GLUTEN-FREE PUMPKIN SOUR
CREAM PANCAKES

64

WILD RICE AND OAT FLOURLESS
PUMPKIN PANCAKES

67

AVOCADO TOAST WITH PUMPKIN
BUTTER AND SPROUTS

68

SAVORY YOGURT WITH ROASTED
PUMPKIN, BLACK QUINOA,
PUMPKIN SEED PESTO, AND CHILI

71

TOAST WITH PUMPKIN, KALE,
MUSHROOMS, POACHED EGGS,
AND HERB OIL

73

HUEVOS RANCHEROS WITH
SMOKY PUMPKIN SAUCE

75

NO-KNEAD PUMPKIN BREAKFAST
BRAIDS

77

PUMPKIN GINGER BREAD WITH
DARK CHOCOLATE AND COCONUT

78

MORNING GLORY PUMPKIN
MUFFINS

81

SHARP CHEDDAR, PUMPKIN, AND
PECAN SCONES

82

SPICED PUMPKIN OATMEAL WITH BAKED PEARS AND PECANS

When the mercury dips—even ever so slightly—I return to the warming breakfasts of fall and winter that hold the unique ability to serve as both aromatherapy and sustenance. The moment the pat of butter hits the heat and coats tawny, nutty steel-cut oats, the kitchen fills with the most delectable oatmeal cookie aroma, acting as a gentle wake-up call for the chillier weather (and for yourself). Pumpkin purée adds depth, sweetness, and volume, playing nicely off maple-like pecans and cozy roasted pears.

This recipe can be made completely ahead, allowing you to quickly prepare steel-cut oats on a weekday with a rapid reheat.

.... *Serves 4–6* ....

4 pears, halved and cored (they can even be a little under-ripe)

1 tablespoon unsalted butter

1 cup steel-cut oats

4 cups milk of choice, plus more for serving

2 cups pumpkin purée

¼ cup demerara sugar (dark brown sugar) or maple syrup, plus more for serving

1½ teaspoons pumpkin spice (see page **247**)

¾ teaspoon salt

⅓ cup chopped pecans

Preheat oven to 350°F. Add pears, cut-side down on a parchment-lined baking sheet. Bake for 20 to 30 minutes, until very soft when pierced with a knife. Meanwhile, make the oatmeal.

In a large pot, melt butter over medium-high. Add oats and toast for 1 minute, stirring constantly, until fragrant. Stir in remaining oatmeal ingredients except pecans, bring to a boil, reduce to medium-low, and cook, uncovered, stirring often for 25 to 30 minutes. Oats should be tender and porridge should be thick. Scoop into bowls and top each serving with a baked pear and sprinkle of pecans. Serve with additional milk and brown sugar or maple syrup.

SAVORY HERBED PUMPKIN OATMEAL
WITH SOFT-BOILED EGGS AND PUMPKIN SEED PESTO

Oats, much like rice, are a grain, and they're even prepared similar to risotto, making them a model candidate for the savory flavors I've employed here. Instead of pine nuts and basil, a verdant swirl of pesto made with arugula and pumpkin seeds awakens the taste buds with a peppery bite, contrasting an herby pillow of oats and a meltingly luxurious soft-boiled egg. It's a cozy, hearty breakfast that will make you a cold weather convert at first spoonful.

Serves 4–6

For the Savory Herbed Pumpkin Oatmeal

1 tablespoon unsalted butter

1 cup steel-cut oats

4 cups milk of choice, plus more for serving

2 cups pumpkin purée

1 tablespoon fresh sage, finely chopped, plus more for serving

¾ teaspoon salt

4–6 eggs

ground black pepper, to taste

For the Pumpkin Seed Pesto

1 clove garlic, peeled

½ cup raw, unsalted green pumpkin seeds

2 cups packed arugula

⅓ cup pumpkin seed oil or extra-virgin olive oil

2 tablespoons lemon juice

½ teaspoon salt

In a large pot, melt butter over medium-high heat. Add oats and toast for 1 minute, stirring constantly, until fragrant. Stir in remaining oatmeal ingredients, except eggs. Bring to a boil, reduce heat to medium-low, and cook, uncovered, stirring often for 25 to 30 minutes. Oats should be tender and porridge should be thick. Meanwhile, make the pesto.

In a food processor, pulse garlic until minced. Add pumpkin seeds and arugula and blend until finely chopped. Add oil, lemon juice, and salt, and blend until smooth. Store in an airtight jar in the refrigerator for up to 2 weeks or freeze for up to 3 months.

Fill a medium saucepan with 4 to 6 inches of water (enough so eggs will be fully submerged. Bring to a boil. Gently add eggs and continue to boil for 6 minutes and 30 seconds. Drain and rinse with cold water. Gently tap and peel to remove shell.

Scoop oats into bowls, swirl in spoonful of pesto, and top with a soft-boiled egg (halve directly in bowl with a sharp knife to prevent the yolk from running). Serve with ground black pepper and additional sage.

PUMPKIN PIE GRANOLA WITH PECANS

My granola is famous within my family, and the formula is both simple and highly adaptable. The secret is a slow bake in a low oven with absolutely no stirring. Your home will be filled with a scrumptious, spiced pecan pie aroma for hours as it bakes and cools, making you count the minutes until your first nibble.

Makes about 4 cups

⅓ cup coconut oil, melted
⅓ cup maple syrup
1 teaspoon vanilla extract
3 cups large-flake rolled oats (not instant)
1 cup chopped pecans
2 tablespoons packed demerara sugar (dark brown sugar)
1 tablespoon plus 1 teaspoon pumpkin spice (see page **247**)
¾ teaspoon sea salt

Preheat oven to 300°F. Line a large-rimmed baking sheet with parchment paper.

In a large bowl, combine coconut oil, maple syrup, and vanilla. Mix in remaining ingredients. Spread evenly onto prepared baking sheet and bake for 1 hour, until uniformly browned. Cool completely on baking sheet before storing airtight in the pantry. Serve with yogurt, milk, or enjoy by the handful.

SUPER-SEED PUMPKIN SPICE AND APPLE MUESLI

A year-round favorite of mine, make-ahead muesli is packed with nutritious goodies, and this one gets a super-booster from a stellar seed mix. Pumpkin, hemp, and chia seeds provide protein, iron, fiber, and healthy fats for the ultimate morning power meal. This keeps for 1 week in the refrigerator.

.... *Serves 6* ....

2 cups large-flake rolled oats (not instant)
½ cup raw, unsalted green pumpkin seeds
¼ cup hulled hemp seeds (hemp hearts)
1 tablespoon chia seeds
½ teaspoon pumpkin spice (see page **247**)
½ teaspoon salt
1 cup buttermilk or kefir
1 cup water
1–2 tablespoons maple syrup (use full amount for a sweeter muesli)
1 tablespoon lemon juice
1 teaspoon vanilla extract
1 apple, any variety, grated
pomegranate arils or fresh berries, for serving

In a large bowl, combine oats, pumpkin seeds, hemp seeds, chia seeds, pumpkin spice, and salt. In a medium bowl, combine buttermilk or kefir, water, maple syrup, lemon juice, and vanilla; stir into oat mixture, followed by apple. Cover and refrigerate for at least 4 hours, preferably overnight. Stir and serve with pomegranate or berries on top.

SHAKSHUKA WITH PUMPKIN AND PEPPERS

Life, like cooking breakfast, can be given a helping hand with a bit of planning ahead, be that an engagement or meal, respectively. I can't imagine standing at a stove, stirring peppers and onions at 8 o'clock in the morning, which is exactly why I always make shakshuka's crimson, heady sauce (without the eggs) ahead of time to store in the refrigerator or freezer. Pumpkin is a new addition to this traditional North African recipe, lending a bit of sturdiness for the eggs to poach away in, while getting thick and sticky-sweet in the oven.

Serves 4

2 tablespoons extra-virgin olive oil

2 red bell peppers, halved, seeded, and thinly sliced

1 onion, thinly sliced

4 cloves garlic, minced

2 teaspoons caraway seeds

2 teaspoons ground cumin

1 teaspoon smoked paprika or mild Hungarian paprika

1 teaspoon salt

¼ teaspoon chili flakes

1½ cups pumpkin purée

2 tablespoons apple cider vinegar

4 large eggs

herbs, freshly chopped, for serving

Preheat oven to 375°F.

In a large skillet, warm oil over medium heat. Add bell peppers, onion, garlic, caraway, cumin, paprika, salt, and chili flakes. Reduce heat to medium-low; sauté for 10–12 minutes, until vegetables are soft. Stir in pumpkin and vinegar. Remove from heat and create four shallow holes; crack eggs into holes. Bake for 10 to 15 minutes, or until eggs are set (keep an eye on them to cook to your liking). Using an oven mitt, remove shakshuka from oven, sprinkle herbs on top, and serve.

NOTES

For single servings, before adding eggs and baking, portion cooked vegetables into ovenproof ramekins or dishes; create a shallow hole in each and crack in an egg. Bake according to directions for large skillet.

GLUTEN-FREE PUMPKIN SOUR CREAM PANCAKES

Gluten-free or otherwise, I much prefer these fluffy, pancake house–style pancakes to the old-school version made with white flour. Impossibly burnished on the outside, tender on the inside, they're tasty enough to eat plain thanks to the belle of the ball—pumpkin— lending its trademark earthy sweetness and breathtaking sunset-orange hue. If you enjoy your pancakes with maple syrup, as I usually do, I like to keep it on the side with these and dunk each piece—it's messy and greedy and the perfect way to enjoy a pancake that feels this special.

To reheat leftovers (in the unlikely event you have some), pop them in the toaster for a fresh-from-the-pan crispiness at the speed of light. And yes, this means pancakes on a workday.

Makes 6–8 large pancakes

1¾ cups oat flour (purchase or make by blending 2 cups quick-cooking rolled oats in a blender or food processor until a fine flour forms)

2 tablespoons coconut sugar or evaporated cane sugar

2 teaspoons baking powder

½ teaspoon pumpkin spice (see page **247**) or ground cinnamon

¼ teaspoon salt

1 cup milk of choice

½ cup pumpkin purée

¼ cup full-fat sour cream, plus more for serving

1 large egg

oil or unsalted butter, for cooking

Preheat oven to 200°F. Line a large-rimmed baking sheet with parchment paper.

In a large bowl, combine flour, sugar, baking powder, pumpkin spice or cinnamon, and salt. In a medium bowl, whisk together milk, pumpkin, sour cream, and egg; add to flour mixture and whisk together.

Preheat a large nonstick skillet or nonstick griddle pan to medium. Add a thin layer of oil or butter. Ladle pancake batter into pan; cook for 2 to 3 minutes per side. Transfer to prepared baking sheet and keep warm in oven until ready to serve. Repeat with remaining batter, adding a thin layer of oil or butter with each batch for cooking. Serve warm with additional sour cream and maple syrup.

> **NOTES**
>
> Before flipping, add a few blueberries, chocolate chips, dried cranberries, banana slices, or walnut pieces, if you like.

WILD RICE AND OAT FLOURLESS PUMPKIN PANCAKES

Don't expect a light and fluffy pancake like the previous recipe; this is a stack of hearty, healthy sustenance for cold weather. Restyle for a savory take with steamed spinach (see *Notes*) and a poached or fried egg, or keep it classically sweet with a river of maple syrup and pat of butter. How you adorn these griddlecakes is really up to you—peanut butter, jam, yogurt, banana slices, and whipped cream all come to mind as fair partners (likely best not all at once though).

You'll need to cook the wild rice ahead, which may seem fussy, but you may cook the pancakes entirely ahead, as well. Once cooked, individually freeze pancakes on a parchment-lined baking sheet, store in a zip-top bag in the freezer, and reheat in the oven when you're ready to enjoy. With no flour or wheat to hold everything together tightly, these pancakes are delicate (but gluten-free); a gentle hand rules the griddlecake pan. Be careful and confident when flipping.

Makes 5–6 pancakes

1 cup pumpkin purée

2 large eggs

1 teaspoon vanilla

1⅓ cups cooked wild rice (see *Notes*)

½ cup large-flake rolled oats (not instant)

½ teaspoon baking soda

¼ teaspoon ground nutmeg

¼ teaspoon salt

oil or unsalted butter for cooking, plus more for serving

maple syrup, for serving

Preheat oven to 200°F. Line a large-rimmed baking sheet with parchment paper. In a large bowl, mix pumpkin, eggs, and vanilla. Mix in remaining ingredients until well combined. Rest batter for 5 minutes.

To cook pancakes, heat a large nonstick griddle or nonstick skillet to medium; wipe a thin layer of oil or butter. Scoop ⅓ to ½ cup portions of batter on pan, smoothing into a ½-inch high round. Cook for 3 to 4 minutes, carefully flip, and cook for 2 minutes longer. Transfer to prepared baking sheet and keep warm in oven until ready to serve. Repeat with remaining batter, adding a thin layer of oil or butter with each batch for cooking. Serve hot with additional coconut oil or butter and maple syrup.

> **NOTES**
>
> *To cook wild rice:* In a medium saucepan, bring 4 cups water and 1 cup wild rice to a boil. Reduce to a simmer, partially cover, and cook for 40 to 50 minutes, until tender and grains are burst. Drain into a fine mesh sieve and measure out amount as per recipe instructions. Use leftover wild rice in salads, oatmeal, burgers, quick breads, muffins, or as a fast side dish with a touch of butter and salt.

AVOCADO TOAST WITH PUMPKIN BUTTER AND SPROUTS

No longer just for the summer months, this is a new breed of avocado toast that will take you into the chillier weather. Pumpkin butter shows its versatility as an ochre-hued, perfectly sweet and spicy bedding for velvety slices of avocado. This toast pairs well with a piping hot coffee or tea for a substantial yet healthy start to your day.

The pumpkin butter is made in the slow cooker, requiring a little planning ahead. Make it the day before to refrigerate, or whip it up weeks in advance to freeze. Many other ideas in these pages will help to use up your batch of pumpkin butter beyond toast, though off the spoon is more than good enough for me.

.... *Serves 1* ....

1–2 slices whole grain bread, preferably rustic-style, one with plenty of seeds
¼ cup Pumpkin Butter (see page **248**)
½ avocado, pitted, peeled, and thinly sliced
sprouts
cilantro
salt, to taste

Toast bread and spread with a thick layer of pumpkin butter. Top with avocado, sprouts, cilantro, and salt. Serve.

SAVORY YOGURT WITH ROASTED PUMPKIN, BLACK QUINOA, PUMPKIN SEED PESTO, AND CHILI

Containing a decidedly Halloween-esque spectrum of colors with raven quinoa, edible jack-o-lantern, spooky green pesto paint splotches, and blood-red chili flecks, this is a meal as vibrant tasting as it is looking. And, savory yogurt is quite trendy as of this writing, so you can not only impress diners with your cutting-edge cuisine, but give them a little scare, too.

Serves 4

1 (2–3 pound) creamy-fleshed pumpkin such as red kuri, seeded, peeled, and cut into ½-inch cubes or thin wedges
1 tablespoon extra-virgin olive oil, plus more for brushing
salt, to taste
½ cup black or white quinoa
2 cups plain whole milk yogurt
½ chili, minced
¼ cup Pumpkin Seed Pesto (see page **56**)

Preheat oven to 375°F. On a large-rimmed baking sheet, toss pumpkin with oil and salt, to taste. Roast for 30 to 35 minutes until tender. Use warm or chilled. Meanwhile, cook quinoa.

Bring quinoa and water to a boil, reduce to a simmer, cover, and cook for 15 minutes. Remove from heat and steam, covered, for 5 minutes. Fluff with a fork and use warm or chilled.

To serve, add ½ cup yogurt to each bowl, top with sections of quinoa and squash, spoon over pesto, and sprinkle with chili. Serve warm or chilled. These can even be assembled and refrigerated overnight.

TOAST WITH PUMPKIN, KALE, MUSHROOMS, POACHED EGGS, AND HERB OIL

Serving this forest feast as a late breakfast or brunch (I've even enjoyed it for dinner) is just what you'll want to tuck into after a crisp fall morning walk or bitterly cold winter driveway-shoveling session.

.... *Serves 1* ....

For the Herb Oil (optional)
2 large sprigs fresh rosemary
5 large sprigs fresh thyme, plus more for serving
1 cup extra-virgin olive oil

For the Toast
1 tablespoon Herb Oil or extra-virgin olive oil, divided
1 portobello mushroom, sliced into ¼-inch pieces
1 clove garlic, minced
¼ teaspoon fresh or dried thyme, chopped

4 leaves lacinato kale, de-stemmed, torn into bite-sized pieces
¼ cup Pumpkin Butter (see page **248**)
1 teaspoon apple cider vinegar
salt, to taste
1 tablespoon distilled white vinegar
1 egg
1–2 slices whole grain bread, preferably rustic-style, one with plenty of seeds
Smoky Roasted Pumpkin Seeds (see page **252**) (optional)

For the herb oil (if making) in a medium, clean glass jar, stuff herbs in the bottom and cover with oil. Make sure herbs are fully submerged to avoid mold. Tightly seal and place in a cool, dark place for 5 days. Strain through a fine mesh sieve and discard herbs. Store herb oil in an airtight glass jar in the pantry for up to 1 year.

In a medium, nonstick skillet or cast-iron skillet, heat 2 teaspoons herb oil or extra-virgin olive oil over medium heat. Add mushrooms in a single layer and fry on first side for 3 to 5 minutes, until a golden crust develops on bottom side. Flip mushrooms, stir in garlic and thyme, followed by kale; season with salt. Cook until kale is wilted and mushrooms are tender. Keep warm.

In a separate small skillet or small saucepan over medium heat, warm pumpkin butter with apple cider vinegar and remaining 1 teaspoon herb oil or extra-virgin olive oil; season with salt. Keep warm.

To poach the egg, fill a small saucepan with 3 to 4 inches of water and distilled white vinegar; bring to a simmer. Crack egg into a ramekin and carefully slip into simmering water. Continue to simmer for 1 minute, remove from heat, cover, and let stand off heat for 4 minutes. Use a slotted spoon to remove egg from water when serving. Meanwhile, toast your bread.

To assemble, spread toast with warmed pumpkin mixture, and top with mushrooms, kale, poached egg, and pumpkin seeds, if using.

HUEVOS RANCHEROS WITH SMOKY PUMPKIN SAUCE

Truth be told, I'd never had huevos rancheros until I worked on this recipe. In the United States, it appears to be quite popular, but in Canada? Not so much (at least, it wasn't in the small, Canadian countryside town I grew up in). Huevos rancheros seemed fussy and complicated, which is certainly not something I'd consider making bleary-eyed first thing in the morning; I actually prefer this for lunch or dinner, but this recipe appears in the breakfast chapter for nomenclature's sake. Pumpkin purée is a non-traditional addition, but adds body and a delicate sweetness to the sauce without an overarching squash taste. I'm confounded by how simple this is to make. It's ready in about 30 minutes, too.

Serves 4

4 (6-inch) corn tortillas

1 (19-ounce) can black beans or 2 cups cooked black beans, drained and rinsed if using canned

2 avocados, halved, pitted, peeled, and thinly sliced

4 eggs

refined avocado oil or extra-virgin olive oil, for frying eggs

1 jalapeño, thinly sliced

1 lime, quartered

For the Smoky Pumpkin Sauce

1 cup pumpkin purée

¼ cup tomato paste

1 tablespoon apple cider vinegar

1 tablespoon refined avocado oil or extra-virgin olive oil

1 teaspoon ground cumin

1 teaspoon smoked paprika

½ teaspoon granulated dried garlic or 1 clove fresh garlic, minced

½ teaspoon salt

¼ teaspoon chili flakes

Preheat oven to 400°F. To make the tortilla "bowls," gently press tortillas into an ovenproof bowl or wide ramekin; place a smaller ovenproof bowl or smaller ramekin in the center to help it hold its shape. (You can also crisp them flat on a baking sheet if you don't want to mold them into a bowl shape.) Bake for 12 to 15 minutes, until edges brown and tortilla holds its shape. Using oven mitts or a dry kitchen towel, remove bowls or ramekins and place tortilla "bowls" in serving bowls or on serving plates. Set aside.

For the sauce, combine all sauce ingredients in a medium saucepan and warm over medium heat, stirring often, until garlic is cooked through and sauce is hot.

Warm beans in a medium saucepan or very briefly in the microwave, and fry eggs to desired cook.

To assemble, fill each tortilla "bowl" with warmed black beans, a fan of avocado, dollop of sauce, and top with a fried egg. Garnish with jalapeño and lime wedges. Serve immediately.

NO-KNEAD PUMPKIN BREAKFAST BRAIDS

If you'd like, make the dough the night before, refrigerate, and bring to room temperature to serve them warm for your holiday breakfast. Or, bake them all up and freeze in zip-top bags. These are my preferred alternatives to cinnamon buns on the Day family Christmas morning breakfast table.

Makes 16

¼ cup warm water

1 tablespoon quick-rise yeast

1 cup 2% or whole milk, plus more for brushing

½ cup unsalted butter

¾ cup pumpkin purée

⅓ cup lightly packed light brown sugar

1 teaspoon pumpkin spice (see page **247**)

1 teaspoon salt

3½ cups unbleached all-purpose flour

1½ cups whole wheat pastry flour

seeds or coarse sugar for sprinkling (optional)

In a small bowl, combine water and yeast. Let sit until foamy (about 5 minutes).

In a medium saucepan, combine milk and butter over medium heat until butter is melted. Add to a large mixing bowl along with pumpkin and brown sugar; whisk to combine. Let cool until just warm. Stir in yeast mixture, pumpkin spice, and salt. Stir in flours all at once; mix until fully combined (using your hands may be helpful). It should be sticky yet dry to the touch; if the dough looks wet, add additional all-purpose flour a small amount at a time. Cover with a kitchen towel and set in a warm spot away from drafts to proof for 3 hours, until doubled in volume.

Line two large-rimmed baking sheets with parchment paper. Punch down dough and dump onto a lightly floured clean countertop. Slice into 16 equal pieces (cut into quarters, then cut each quarter into quarters). Working one at a time, roll a piece of dough into a long log; slice into 3 equal pieces; pinch the pieces together at the top and braid. Tuck under any stray pieces and pinch the bottom to seal. Place on prepared baking sheet, leaving 2 inches per braid. Repeat with remaining dough. Cover both baking sheets loosely with a kitchen towel and proof for 30 minutes.

Arrange oven racks to accommodate two baking sheets. Preheat oven to 375°F. Brush braids with additional milk and sprinkle with seeds or coarse sugar, if using. Bake for 10 minutes, rotate baking sheets, and bake for an additional 10 to 15 minutes, until golden and puffed. Enjoy warm out of the oven or cool. Store in an airtight container or zip-top bag at room temperature or freeze for up to 1 month. Reheat braids in a low oven to warm.

PUMPKIN GINGER BREAD WITH DARK CHOCOLATE AND COCONUT

In my university days, I would stop at a rather omnipresent coffee shop—I think you can guess which one—after a day of classes and buy a slice of pumpkin bread and chai latté. It was my weekday ritual, and one that I looked forward to immensely. (It's quite unnerving to think I could have had a hefty down payment on a house with the amount of money I spent on my afterschool snacks.) Nearly a decade later and pumpkin bread still does it for me, with this loaf being no exception. I prefer the slice cold, straight out of the refrigerator with the chocolate set, cracking off into shards and melting in my mouth with each bite. I will suggest you enjoy this with a latté or strong cup of tea for best results and warm, fuzzy feelings.

Makes 1 loaf

2 cups light spelt flour

1 tablespoon baking powder

2 teaspoons ground dried ginger

¼ teaspoon grated nutmeg

½ teaspoon salt

1 cup pumpkin purée

½ cup milk of choice

⅓ cup evaporated cane sugar

¼ cup coconut oil, melted

2 tablespoons molasses

1 large egg

1 teaspoon apple cider vinegar

4 ounces (heaping ½ cup) chopped dark chocolate or dark chocolate chips, melted

¼ cup unsweetened coconut chips or unsweetened shredded coconut

Preheat oven to 350°F. Line a standard loaf pan (9 x 5 inches) with parchment paper, leaving some overhang for easy removal.

In a large bowl, combine flour, baking powder, ginger, nutmeg, and salt. In a medium bowl, combine pumpkin, milk, sugar, oil, molasses, egg, and vinegar. Add pumpkin mixture into flour mixture and stir until combined. Transfer batter to prepared loaf pan, smooth top, and bake for 40 to 55 minutes, until a toothpick inserted in the center comes out clean. Cool in pan for 5 minutes. Run a knife around the loaf to release any pieces clinging to the pan and transfer to a wire cooling rack using the parchment overhang. Cool completely.

After bread is completely cool, spread melted chocolate and sprinkle coconut. Allow chocolate to set (about 4 hours) before slicing and serving. Store airtight in the refrigerator.

MORNING GLORY PUMPKIN MUFFINS

Detour, a fabulous café near my home in Hamilton, Ontario, Canada, has the ultimate morning glory muffin; I can't stop in there without picking one up, and I usually make sure everyone I bring there tries it, too. My recipe is not a duplicate of this fabulous morning glory muffin, but a pumpkin-filled homage. Moist, tender, not overly sweet, filled with fruit and seeds, and ideal with a cup of strong coffee, they're the official grab-and-go breakfast or mid-afternoon snack of champions.

.... *Makes 14–16 large muffins* ....

2 cups light spelt flour

2 teaspoons baking powder

1 teaspoon baking soda

1 teaspoon ground cinnamon

½ teaspoon salt

2 large eggs

2 ripe bananas, mashed

¾ cup pumpkin purée

½ cup evaporated cane sugar or granulated sugar

½ cup neutral-tasting oil

2 teaspoons vanilla extract

1 apple, any variety, grated

⅔ cup raw, unsalted green pumpkin seeds

½ cup golden raisins or sultana raisins

2 tablespoons sesame seeds

1 tablespoon poppy seeds

Preheat oven to 350°F. Line two standard muffin tins with large muffin papers (you'll only need 14 to 16 large muffin papers).

In a medium bowl, combine flour, baking powder, baking soda, cinnamon, and salt. In a large bowl, whisk eggs, banana, pumpkin, sugar, oil, and vanilla until mixed. Stir dry mixture into wet mixture until just combined. Fold in apple, seeds, and raisins.

Scoop heaped ¼ cup (about 5 tablespoons) portions into muffin papers. Bake for 22 to 28 minutes, until a toothpick inserted in the center comes out clean. Transfer to a wire rack to cool completely. Store airtight in refrigerator for up to 2 weeks, or freeze in a zip-top bag for up to 2 months. (Defrost at room temperature before eating.)

SHARP CHEDDAR, PUMPKIN, AND PECAN SCONES

Scones are best made fresh, making a homemade version essential. With so many baked goods being, for the most part, exceptional when store-bought these days, it's nice to have an outlier. Scones are this outlier. This recipe is a cinch to prepare, especially if you use a food processor, and can be made ahead and baked to order when you need them in the morning. For serving, I can see these pumpkin patch orange, sweet-savory biscuits as part of a holiday brunch. Or, take the tray back to bed and feed yourself warm scones in the morning with coffee. They're good any way, really.

Makes 18–20

2 cups light spelt flour, plus more for rolling
3 tablespoons light brown sugar, packed
1 tablespoon baking powder
½ teaspoon salt
¼ teaspoon ground nutmeg

6 tablespoons unsalted butter, cubed, very cold
1 cup pumpkin purée
2 ounces sharp (mature) cheddar, grated (heaping ½ cup grated)
½ cup chopped pecans
milk, for brushing

In a food processor or large bowl by hand, pulse or mix to combine flour, sugar, baking powder, salt, and nutmeg. Pulse or cut in butter until mixture resembles a coarse meal. Blend or stir in pumpkin. Pulse or stir in cheddar and pecans.

Lightly flour a clean countertop and dump out dough. Form into a round. Using a floured rolling pin, roll dough into a large circle ½ inch high. With a 2½- to 3-inch cookie cutter or drinking glass rim, cut rounds and place 2 inches apart on a large-rimmed baking sheet. Gather dough scraps, re-roll, and repeat (you will need two baking sheets). Lightly brush top of scones with milk.

Bake for 12 to 15 minutes, until puffed and bottoms are golden brown. While first batch of scones is baking, refrigerate other tray. Bake second tray of scones. Cool completely on baking sheet. Serve warm or at room temperature. Keep leftover scones in a covered glass or ceramic dish at room temperature.

NOTES

These scones taste best the day they're made. To make ahead, prepare recipe up until scones are brushed with milk. In the morning, brush scones with milk and bake.

SOUPS

In the fall and winter months (and sometimes even in the summer), I'm so easily drawn to a steaming, fragrant bowl of soup. From puréed to broth-based to decadently rich, soup is the ultimate cold weather luxury and emotional pacifier. Beginning with a strong base, aggressive seasonings, and, in this case, the right variety of pumpkin for the job, soups inspired from all corners of the world will massage the kinks out of a bad day, warm your bones, and fill you up. With the ability to be puréed into silky submission or stay put as a meaty cube, pumpkin's malleability is showcased at first soupy slurp. Loaded with produce, grains, and legumes, the following chapter is filled with wholesome nourishment for when you need it most.

RECITES

SIMPLE ROASTED PUMPKIN SOUP WITH SMOKY PUMPKIN SEEDS
89

PHO WITH PUMPKIN, SPELT NOODLES, MUSHROOMS, AND TOFU
90

EASY LENTIL SOUP WITH GREENS AND PUMPKIN
93

THAI COCONUT SOUP WITH PUMPKIN, NOODLES, AND LIME
95

SILKY PUMPKIN GINGER SOUP WITH CLEMENTINE AND VANILLA
96

SIMPLE ROASTED PUMPKIN SOUP WITH SMOKY ROASTED PUMPKIN SEEDS

During the cold weather, my motto is that any vegetable that can be puréed, will be puréed. And no vegetable does such a good job of blending into silky, soupy submission quite like the pumpkin. Its subtle sweetness shines through with each bite, balancing savory onion, forest-like sage, and a smoky pumpkin seed garnish. Often, when I eat vegetable soups, I never feel entirely satisfied; soup is always the partner of something heartier, but this deeply rich one carries me through even the most active, blustery fall and winter afternoons.

Serves 4–6

1 (2–3 pound) sugar pumpkin or other small roasting pumpkin, peeled, seeds reserved, and cut into rough pieces

1 onion, peeled and cut into rough pieces

3 cloves garlic, peeled, left whole

8 whole fresh sage leaves

2 tablespoons extra-virgin olive oil

1 teaspoon salt

ground black pepper, to taste

3 cups low-sodium vegetable stock

2 tablespoons 35% heavy whipping cream or full-fat coconut milk, plus more for serving

Smoky Roasted Pumpkin Seeds (see page **252**), for serving

Preheat oven to 375°F. On a large-rimmed baking sheet, toss pumpkin, onion, garlic, and sage with oil, salt, and pepper. Roast for 45 minutes. Transfer vegetables to a blender or large pot for blending with an immersion blender, along with stock and cream (if your blender jug is small, you may need to do this in batches); blend until smooth. Transfer to a large pot to heat over medium, stirring often, until very hot. Serve with a swirl of cream and sprinkle of pumpkin seeds.

NOTES

If you prefer a thinner soup, add vegetable stock ½ cup at a time until desired consistency.

Soup can be frozen for up to 3 months.

PHO WITH PUMPKIN, SPELT NOODLES, MUSHROOMS, AND TOFU

Pumpkin goes so well with the cinnamony spices pho is known for, making it the perfect match for this heady, complete-meal broth bowl.

.... *Serves 4* ....

For the Pumpkin

1 (2–3 pound) creamy-fleshed pumpkin such as red kuri, seeded, peeled, and cut into ½-inch cubes or thin wedges

1 tablespoon toasted sesame oil or extra-virgin olive oil

For the Broth

6 cups water

4 cloves garlic, minced

4 tablespoons brown rice miso or mellow white miso

2 tablespoons maple syrup

2 tablespoons unseasoned rice vinegar

2 tablespoons tamari

1 (2-inch) piece ginger, peeled, left whole

4 whole star anise

2 cinnamon sticks

½ teaspoon chili flakes or ½ fresh red chili, minced

4 portobello mushrooms, thinly sliced

For Serving

8 ounces spelt spaghetti, cooked, drained, rinsed with cold water, drained again, room temperature

1 (12-ounce) package extra-firm tofu, pressed if you have time, sliced into thin matchsticks or cubed, room temperature

1 small bunch cilantro, roughly chopped

2 teaspoons sesame seeds

Preheat oven to 375°F. On a large-rimmed baking sheet, toss pumpkin with oil. Roast for 30 to 35 minutes, or until tender.

For the broth, in a large saucepan, slowly whisk water into garlic, miso, maple syrup, vinegar, and tamari until fully combined. Mix in ginger, star anise, cinnamon, chili, and mushrooms. Bring to a gentle simmer over medium-high heat, cover, reduce to low, and simmer for 20 minutes. Discard ginger, star anise, and cinnamon stick.

Ladle hot broth (including mushrooms) into very large, deep bowls. Top with sections of noodles, pumpkin, tofu, and cilantro. Sprinkle with sesame seeds and serve.

EASY LENTIL SOUP WITH GREENS AND PUMPKIN

In late fall and winter, I like to keep lentil soup in the refrigerator for quick, healthy lunches or dinners. To keep the soup from looking drab (as lentil soups can), along with imparting more nutrition and overall character, lacinato kale and fat cubes of pumpkin are just the boosters this meal needs.

Serves 4

4½ cups water or low-sodium vegetable stock
1 pound (½ of 1 regular) creamy-fleshed pumpkin
    such as kabocha, peeled, seeded, and cut into 1-inch pieces
1 onion, diced
2 cloves garlic, minced
¾ cup uncooked brown lentils
2 tablespoons extra-virgin olive oil
1 tablespoon red wine vinegar
1½ teaspoons salt
1 teaspoon dried thyme
ground black pepper, to taste
4 cups packed, shredded kale or sturdy greens of choice

In a large pot, combine all ingredients except kale. Bring to a boil, reduce to a simmer, cover, and cook for 30 minutes, until lentils are cooked and pumpkin is tender. Stir in kale and cook until wilted and dark green. Serve.

THAI COCONUT SOUP WITH PUMPKIN, NOODLES, AND LIME

There's nothing I love more on a Friday night after a busy week than slurping back a hot, spicy, creamy coconut bowl of soup from a local Thai restaurant. I've done my best to recreate the classic (or, at least, new-classic North American–style) Thai coconut soup here. Pumpkin acts like a sponge, soaking up every essence of the broth; ditto the tangle of noodles.

Serves 3–4

1 tablespoon coconut oil

1 pound (½ of 1 regular) red kuri pumpkin, peeled, seeded, and cut into 1-inch pieces

½ pound (1 large or 2 small) Japanese eggplant, cut into 1-inch half-rounds

2 cloves garlic, minced

1 fresh red chili, minced

zest of 1 lime

1 teaspoon salt

2 cups water

1 (14-ounce) can full-fat coconut milk

2 tablespoons lime juice

½ pound bok choy, cut into thin wedges or shredded

4–6 ounces whole grain spaghetti or linguini or rice stick noodles, cooked and drained

lime wedges

coconut chips (optional)

tamari

In a large pot, warm oil over medium heat. Add pumpkin and eggplant, stir, cover, and cook for 10 minutes, stirring once or twice, until vegetables begin to brown. Stir in garlic, chili, lime juice, and salt, followed by water, coconut milk, and lime juice. Bring to a boil, reduce to a simmer, cover, and cook for 10 to 15 minutes, until pumpkin is very tender. Stir in bok choy and cook until tender (about 2 minutes).

To deep serving bowls, add noodles; ladle in broth and vegetables. Garnish with lime wedges and a sprinkle of coconut flakes, if using. Serve hot with tamari for seasoning.

SILKY PUMPKIN GINGER SOUP WITH CLEMENTINE AND VANILLA

Vanilla in something savory may seem peculiar, but its spirit comes up from underneath, giving this honeyed, vibrant soup a hint of special-occasion. Floral clementine juice and spicy ginger bring out pumpkin's sweet side, without making it saccharine. If you don't have any of the pumpkin varieties I've listed below, butternut squash will work just as well.

Serves 6–8

1 (2–3 pound) creamy-fleshed pumpkin such as kabocha or red kuri, seeded and halved

1 onion, roughly chopped

1 tablespoon fresh ginger, finely chopped

4 cups low-sodium vegetable stock, divided

¼ cup clementine juice (from 2 clementines) or orange juice

2 tablespoons extra-virgin olive oil

½ teaspoon vanilla extract

½ teaspoon salt, plus more to taste

ground black pepper, to garnish

clementine slices, to garnish (optional)

Preheat oven to 475°F. Line a large-rimmed baking sheet with parchment paper.

Place pumpkin on prepared baking sheet flesh-side down and nestle onion and ginger next to it. Roast for 45 minutes to 1 hour, until pumpkin is tender. Cool until you can comfortably handle it.

Add half of stock, clementine juice, vanilla, salt, and olive oil to a blender. Scoop pumpkin flesh out of skin (discard skin) and place in the blender along with onion and ginger. Blend until smooth and creamy. Transfer to a large pot, add remaining stock, and reheat over medium until hot. Taste and season with additional salt, if desired. Serve hot with ground pepper and clementine slices, if using.

SNACKS

At every holiday gathering during my childhood, my family had a kids' table where I sat, along with my older brother, Stewart, younger sister, Kirsten, and cousin, Ryan, and the adult table, where the parents and grandparents sat and where we were (okay, we felt) forbidden from sitting. The kids' table at my grandparents' (my late mom's parents) was a small round glass top straight out of the 1970s; the seats were white wrought iron with peach floral cushions (matching the peach bathroom down the hall) and in pristine condition, considering their age. On Christmas Day, from the hours of 3 p.m. to 5 p.m., the kids' table was a makeshift appetizer table, covered in store-bought (my grandma didn't make things from scratch) hot apps and snacks, including marble cheddar with salty "vegetable" crackers, mini quiche, sausage puffs, and peculiar cream cheese blends like pineapple and salmon to spread on whatever we liked. It was a hodgepodge and a tradition that, though I've changed the spread entirely to suit my tastes now, is still happening at every family Christmas dinner.

For you, snacks may be midnight home-from-the-bar requisite, afternoon sustenance when lunch just wasn't enough (or worse, skipped), a light lunch to pick at with good friends and conversation, pre-dinner treats at a holiday gathering, or layered and made into a meal. Snacks defy rules, boundaries, and dietary norms—this statement, all the more true when pumpkin is involved. From the hungry to the hangry, this chapter is dedicated to those of us who served hard time at the kids' table.

RECITES

MAPLE ROASTED PUMPKIN CROSTINI WITH AVOCADO, FETA, AND BALSAMIC GLAZE

103

HALLOUMI PUMPKIN PARCELS WITH POMEGRANATE AND BLACK SESAME

104

ROASTED GARLIC PUMPKIN HUMMUS

107

VEGETABLE BROWN RICE SUSHI WITH GINGER PUMPKIN DIPPING SAUCE

108

POPPY SEED PUMPKIN AND MANGO SALAD ROLLS

111

HONEYED PUMPKIN, FIG, AND TAHINI BITES

113

PUMPKIN DEVILED EGGS WITH MAPLE PECAN "BACON"

114

EASY WHOLE WHEAT PUMPKIN FLATBREADS WITH LEMON THYME

117

MAPLE ROASTED PUMPKIN CROSTINI WITH AVOCADO, FETA, AND BALSAMIC GLAZE

Entertaining around the holidays demands a bit of glitz and glamor in the appetizer department; though this shouldn't mean added stress. Fussy, precious, ultra-dainty appetizers are best left for baby showers and wedding parties. Around the holidays, I like to relax (well, as much as humanly possible), make a bit of a mess, and eat a touch more greedily—hearty, rustic crostini check every box on my wish list. These get the tiger tail treatment with reduced balsamic, providing both beauty and a caramel contrast to briny feta, buttery avocado, and earthy maple-roasted pumpkin. Devour these bold bites with a glass of your preferred poison, good company, and a roaring fire.

Serves 6

1 (2–3 pound or ½ of a large) creamy-fleshed pumpkin such as kabocha, halved, seeded, peeled, and cut into 1-inch cubes

1 tablespoon maple syrup

1 tablespoon extra-virgin olive oil, plus more for serving

1 teaspoon fresh rosemary, chopped

¼ teaspoon salt

ground black pepper, to taste

1 cup balsamic vinegar

½ loaf (1–1½ pound) rustic bread of choice, cut into 1-inch slices

2 cloves garlic, peeled and halved

2 avocados, halved, pitted, and thinly sliced

4 ounces feta, roughly crumbled

Preheat oven to 400°F. Line a large-rimmed baking sheet with parchment paper. Add squash, maple syrup, oil, rosemary, salt, and pepper; toss to combine. Roast for 30 to 35 minutes, until squash is tender and beginning to caramelize. Leave oven on. Meanwhile, for the balsamic glaze, add balsamic to a medium saucepan (turn on your oven vent so you don't choke on the vinegar fumes!), bring to a boil, and continue to boil until thick and reduced (stay back!), about 5 to 10 minutes. Remove from heat to rest for a few minutes; transfer balsamic glaze to a heatproof glass jar. Once cool, seal jar and store in the pantry for a couple of years (yes, years).

Line bread up on a clean, large-rimmed baking sheet. Toast in preheated oven until crispy and golden brown (times vary depending on your oven—keep an eye on it). Transfer toasted bread to a large cutting board and rub each slice with garlic, using the crunchy interior as sandpaper to dissolve the garlic. Top bread with roasted pumpkin and mash with a fork. Top mashed pumpkin with avocado, feta, and a drizzle of balsamic glaze. If your bread is large, slice in half with a serrated knife. Transfer crostini to a serving platter. Serve immediately.

HALLOUMI PUMPKIN PARCELS WITH POMEGRANATE AND BLACK SESAME

Baking spring roll wrappers creates a crispy-bottomed, healthier hot appetizer ideal for any holiday gathering. Inspired by the tastes of North Africa, squeaky, salty halloumi is complimented by pomegranate jewels, creamy pumpkin, and savory cumin. Black sesame seeds are the North African, sun-kissed freckles, adding another pop in texture, aesthetic, and taste.

Makes 12

refined avocado oil or extra-virgin olive oil
1 cup pumpkin purée
2 tablespoons lemon juice
1 teaspoon ground cumin
1 cup fresh cilantro or fresh mint, chopped, plus more for serving
1 (8-ounce) package halloumi (halloom), cut into small cubes
¼ cup pomegranate arils
12 rice paper wrappers
black or white sesame seeds

Preheat oven to 425°F. Line a large-rimmed baking sheet with parchment paper and brush with a thin layer of oil.

In a medium bowl, combine pumpkin, lemon juice, and cumin. Mix in cilantro or mint, halloumi, and pomegranate.

To rehydrate rice paper wrappers, soak one wrapper at a time until pliable (this only takes 15 to 30 seconds) in warm water. Place rehydrated wrapper on a large cutting board or countertop. Place approximately 2 heaping tablespoons of mixture in center of wrapper, gently form into a single layer, and fold into a square (be sure not to wrap too tightly or they'll explode out of the sides in the oven). Place squares seam-side down on prepared baking sheet. Repeat with remaining filling and wrappers. Brush tops with oil and lightly sprinkle with black or white sesame seeds. Bake for 20 to 25 minutes, until dry on top and crispy on bottom. Let cool for 3 to 5 minutes. Serve warm with additional cilantro or mint scattered on top.

ROASTED GARLIC PUMPKIN HUMMUS

Pungent raw garlic irons out its wrinkles in the oven, roasted until it loses all structural integrity; pumpkin hummus deserves this extra step, and you do, too.

Serves 8

1 head garlic, halved horizontally

1 (19-ounce) can chickpeas or 2 cups cooked chickpeas, drained and rinsed if using canned

¾ cup pumpkin purée

⅓ cup lemon juice

⅓ cup tahini

1 tablespoon maple syrup

1 tablespoon cumin

½ teaspoon ground dried ginger

½ teaspoon salt

water, as needed

extra-virgin olive oil

poppy seeds and sesame seeds

Preheat oven to 400°F. Wrap head of garlic in a tight ball of foil or parchment paper, place on a baking sheet, and roast for 45 minutes, until soft. Reserve half a head and save the remaining half for another recipe (store leftovers covered in the refrigerator).

In a food processor, combine roasted garlic, chickpeas, pumpkin, lemon juice, tahini, maple syrup, cumin, ginger, and salt. Blend until smooth, scrape down sides, and blend again for 1 minute. If you prefer a looser hummus, add water, 1 tablespoon at a time, blending after each addition. Swirl hummus onto a serving dish, drizzle with a thread of olive oil, and lightly sprinkle with poppy or sesame seeds. Serve room temperature or chilled with pita bread or crudités. Store leftovers in refrigerator for up to 2 weeks.

VEGETABLE BROWN RICE SUSHI WITH GINGER PUMPKIN DIPPING SAUCE

I assure you DIY sushi is not overly complicated. Cooked brown rice, a little vinegar, a sheet of nori, and some veggies just need to be rolled into a plump cigar. If you don't have a sushi mat, hand rolls (sushi cones) are perfect, too. You could easily serve the sushi simply with tamari, but the dipping sauce is what makes this recipe so delicious. The sauce, with the sweet heat of ginger, combined with pumpkin, miso, and honey is curiously moreish. It's similar to a richer, spicier, plum sauce—hold the goopy, syrupy qualities of pre-made versions.

Makes 4 rolls

For the Vegetable Brown Rice Sushi
½ cup uncooked short-grain brown rice
1 cup water
1 tablespoon rice vinegar
4 sheets nori
⅓ of a cucumber, cut lengthwise matchsticks
½ large avocado, peeled, pitted, and sliced
handful fresh cilantro
sesame seeds

For the Ginger Pumpkin Dipping Sauce
½ cup pumpkin purée
¼ cup rice vinegar
2 tablespoons sweet white miso or brown rice miso
2 tablespoons tamari
2 tablespoons water, plus more to thin
1 teaspoon honey
1 teaspoon ground dried ginger
¼ teaspoon chili flakes

In a medium saucepan, combine water and rice. Bring to a boil, reduce to a simmer, cover, and cook for 45 minutes. Remove from heat and steam, covered, for 5 minutes. Stir in vinegar with a fork, slightly mashing the rice. Cool to room temperature or overnight in the refrigerator.

To roll sushi, place a sheet of nori on a sushi mat and top with a thin layer of rice (don't add too much—you may have leftover rice). On the wide bottom edge closest to you, add a line of cucumber, avocado, and cilantro (again, don't add too much). Roll tightly, using sushi mat to help you squish everything together with each turn. Wrap roll in plastic and refrigerate. Repeat with remaining sushi ingredients.

In a medium bowl, combine all sauce ingredients. Thin with additional water, 1 tablespoon at a time, until desired consistency (it should be quite thick).

Unwrap sushi rolls and slice crosswise into rounds with a very sharp knife. Serve with a sprinkle of sesame seeds and dipping sauce on the side.

POPPY SEED PUMPKIN AND MANGO SALAD ROLLS

A refreshingly hydrating, summer weather–quenching snack, salad rolls with double sunshiny yellow produce—pumpkin and mango—taste as vibrant as they look. Even if you can't actually escape the cold weather, you can warm up the flavors in your kitchen with these tropical(ish) treats. And, I think the fetching orange, black, and green color scheme makes these Halloween party-worthy.

Makes 6–8 rolls

½ (2–3 pound) creamy-fleshed pumpkin such as buttercup or kabocha, peeled, seeded, and cut into ¼-inch thick wedges

2 teaspoons coconut oil

1 teaspoon poppy seeds

¼ teaspoon chili flakes

¼ teaspoon salt

1 mango, peeled and cut into matchsticks

½ head tender lettuce such as Boston or Bibb, leaves separated

fresh cilantro

rice paper wrappers

Preheat oven to 400°F. On a large-rimmed baking sheet, toss pumpkin with oil, seeds, chili, and salt. Roast for 15–20 minutes, until tender and beginning to brown. Cool.

Have all roll ingredients ready to go in front of you for easy building, and work on one roll at a time. Fill a large, high-sided skillet with warm water. To rehydrate rice paper wrappers, soak one wrapper at a time until pliable (this only takes 15 to 30 seconds) in warm water. Place rehydrated wrapper on a large cutting board or countertop. At the bottom of each roll, leaving a ½-inch gap to each side, line up a few pieces of roasted pumpkin, mango, a couple lettuce leaves, and a few sprigs of cilantro. Roll like a burrito, tucking in sides as you turn to encase ingredients. Wrap roll in plastic and store in refrigerator. Dry cutting board or countertop and repeat with remaining ingredients. Serve chilled.

HONEYED PUMPKIN, FIG, AND TAHINI BITES

Take advantage of succulent, fresh figs in the fall, as they're one of the few fruits that still appear to have short, seasonal availability. And what grows together, goes together, making honeyed pumpkin boats and luxurious figs a match made in autumnal heaven. Though simple in preparation and ingredients, this Middle Eastern–esque nibble packs a bold bite.

Makes 4

¼ (2–3 pound) sugar pumpkin or other small roasting pumpkin,
    seeded, peeled, and cut into 4 wide wedges
1 tablespoon honey
2 fresh figs, halved
Tahini Yogurt Dressing (see page **124**)
fresh cilantro or mint

Preheat oven to 375°F. Line a medium-rimmed baking sheet with parchment paper. Toss pumpkin with honey to evenly coat and roast for 35 minutes, until tender. Place on a serving plate, top with half a fig per pumpkin wedge, drizzle with dressing, and garnish with cilantro or mint. Serve warm or chilled.

PUMPKIN DEVILED EGGS WITH MAPLE PECAN "BACON"

To modernize this vintage party app, I've adorned the pumpkin-spiked yolks with a crispy, sweet-and-smoky pecan "bacon" garnish, making it feel rather autumnal, too. This recipe easily doubles or triples to serve more guests.

Makes 12 (6 eggs)

For the Pumpkin Deviled Eggs
6 large eggs
3 tablespoons pumpkin purée
2 tablespoons mayonnaise (I prefer Vegenaise)

For the Maple Pecan "Bacon"
½ cup raw pecan halves
1 teaspoon maple syrup
¼ teaspoon smoked paprika
pinch, salt

Place eggs in medium saucepan and fill with water until it reaches 2 inches above eggs. Bring to a rapid boil, remove from heat, cover, and let sit for 12 minutes. Drain, rinse with cold water, and drain again. Refrigerate until eggs are chilled (about 1 hour).

When eggs are cold, peel and halve vertically; pop out yolk into a small bowl and place hollow whites on a serving plate. Vigorously mash eggs with a fork until yolks are smooth. To yolks, stir in pumpkin and mayonnaise and continue to mash until smooth and creamy. Transfer mixture to a zip-top bag with the tip cut off or pastry bag and pipe into hollowed egg whites. Refrigerate until ready to serve.

Preheat oven to 350°F. Line a large-rimmed baking sheet with parchment paper. Toss pecans, maple syrup, smoked paprika, and salt on parchment, spread in a single layer, and bake for 10 to 12 minutes, until deep brown. Cool completely and coarsely chop.

Sprinkle pecan "bacon" over deviled eggs (there may be extra; great for snacking or topping soups and salads) immediately before serving.

NOTES

The deviled eggs and pecans can both be made ahead (1 day and 5 days, respectively), but keep them separate until ready to serve or the pecans will go soggy.

EASY WHOLE WHEAT PUMPKIN FLATBREADS WITH LEMON THYME

These come together in less than 15 minutes and are a match made in heaven for this chapter's Roasted Garlic Pumpkin Hummus (see page **107**).

Makes 8 small flatbreads

1 cup whole wheat pastry flour, plus more for kneading
1 teaspoon fresh lemon or regular thyme, chopped, plus 8 whole stems to garnish
½ teaspoon baking powder
¼ teaspoon salt
3 tablespoons pumpkin purée
2–3 tablespoons water
refined avocado oil, for pan

In a large bowl, combine flour, chopped thyme, baking powder, and salt. Stir in pumpkin. Add 2 tablespoons water and mix until a ragged dough forms; if it looks too dry, add another tablespoon of water. Knead dough on a lightly floured countertop until elastic and springy (about 4 minutes). Cut into 8 equal pieces and squish with your fingers and palms into rough rounds about ⅛ inch thick. Gently press a small thyme stem into center of each flatbread.

Heat a large nonstick skillet over medium high heat; brush very lightly with oil. Cook flatbreads on side with thyme stem (presentation side) for 2 to 3 minutes, or until brown speckles appear and dough begins to dry out. Flip and cook on second side for 1 to 2 minutes longer. Transfer to a plate and serve warm or at room temperature (can be made 2 to 3 hours in advance).

SALADS AND SIDES

For the traditional tri-divided "meat (or tofu) and potatoes" plate, it's indecent to serve without a side dish or salad. I'll gladly sit down to a mélange of side dishes or big (i.e., non-birdlike, meal-sized) salads, becoming utterly lazy about the protein component (thank goodness for poached and fried eggs). Salads and sides can make a satisfying meal by themselves and can make a meal with other components sparkle. They're the bites we go back to for seconds, and are often vegetable-focused, which pleases me. Pumpkin is involved every which way in this chapter, employed as both the star and sidekick. Whether featuring its traffic cone–orange flesh, crunchy pastel green seeds, or evergreen oil, these pumpkin salads and sides have their dukes up and are ready to fight their way to the spotlight.

RECIPES

PUMPKIN CAESAR SALAD WITH
SAGE SOURDOUGH CROUTONS

123

LETTUCE CUPS WITH ORANGE,
CUMIN SEED ROASTED PUMPKIN,
AND TAHINI YOGURT DRESSING

124

ITALIAN PUMPKIN HOLIDAY
SALAD WITH GORGONZOLA AND
CRANBERRY DRESSING

127

DELICATA SQUASH AND ARUGULA
SALAD WITH PUMPKIN SEED OIL
VINAIGRETTE

128

KALE SLAW WITH APPLES, WHITE
CHEDDAR, AND PUMPKIN HONEY
MUSTARD DRESSING

131

ROASTED JARRAHDALE PUMPKIN
AND ONIONS WITH LEMONY
WHIPPED FETA

132

BLACK QUINOA WITH HEIRLOOM
PUMPKIN, CHESTNUTS, AND MINT

135

ROASTED PUMPKIN WITH ONIONS,
POMEGRANATE, AND YOGURT

136

SKILLET PUMPKIN WITH BROWN
BUTTER, HONEY, AND CLEMENTINE

139

MILLET COUSCOUS WITH
ROASTED PARSNIPS, PUMPKIN,
AND MINT

140

WARM WILD RICE WITH SPINACH,
PUMPKIN, AND GRAPES

142

VANILLA ROASTED PUMPKIN
WEDGES

145

TWICE-BAKED MASHED PUMPKIN
AND APPLES WITH PECAN OAT
CRUNCH

146

LEMONY ROASTED BRUSSELS
SPROUTS AND PUMPKIN SEEDS

148

WHOLE ROASTED CINDERELLA
PUMPKIN

151

PUMPKIN CAESAR SALAD WITH SAGE SOURDOUGH CROUTONS

A remarkably easier take on Caesar salad dressing that walks the line between cream-based and vinaigrette variations, pumpkin purée acts in lieu of raw egg yolks, emulsifying the dressing while keeping things bright—in both texture and color—and light.

Serves 4

For the Sage Sourdough Croutons

4 (1-inch) slices grainy sourdough bread, cut into large cubes

4 teaspoons extra-virgin olive oil

2 teaspoons dried sage

¼ teaspoon salt

ground black pepper, to taste

For the dressing and salad

½ cup pumpkin purée

¼ cup extra-virgin olive oil

¼ cup lemon juice

1 tablespoon Worcestershire sauce (vegan and gluten-free, if required)

¼ teaspoon salt

coarsely ground black pepper, to taste

1 head romaine lettuce, torn into bite-sized pieces or left whole to enjoy with a knife and fork

Preheat oven to 375°F. On a large-rimmed baking sheet, toss all crouton ingredients until evenly coated. Bake for 5 minutes, toss, and bake for 5 to 10 minutes longer, until light brown and crisped. Set aside.

In a small bowl, mix all dressing ingredients.

If tossing salad, combine romaine, croutons, and dressing. Serve immediately. If enjoying with a knife and fork, mound whole romaine leaves on a plate, drizzle with dressing, and top with croutons. Serve immediately.

LETTUCE CUPS WITH ORANGE, CUMIN SEED ROASTED PUMPKIN, AND TAHINI YOGURT DRESSING

Tender lettuce cups act in loco taco, cradling fragrant cumin-crusted pumpkin and juicy orange. A Middle Eastern–inspired combination of flavors capped with a bright tahini yogurt dressing works as an appetizer (move over, crudités), side dish, or light main course for you and a lucky diner.

.... *Serves 4 as a side, 2 as a main* ....

For the Lettuce Cups

1 hooligan pumpkin or ½ (2–3 pound) roasting pumpkin, peeled, seeded, and cut into ½-inch pieces

1 tablespoon extra-virgin olive oil

2 teaspoons whole cumin seed

¼ teaspoon salt

1 head tender lettuce leaves, such as Boston or Bibb

1 navel orange, peeled, and cut into ½-inch pieces

fresh cilantro or mint

For the Tahini Yogurt Dressing

½ cup whole milk yogurt, plain

2 tablespoons tahini

2 tablespoons lemon juice

1 clove garlic, minced

¼ teaspoon salt

Preheat oven to 375°F. On a large-rimmed baking sheet toss pumpkin with oil, cumin seed, and salt. Roast for 35 minutes, until tender and beginning to brown.

In a medium bowl, whisk all dressing ingredients until combined. Refrigerate until ready to serve.

Place lettuce leaves "cuppy"-side up on a large platter; fill with orange pieces and roasted squash. Drizzle cups lightly with dressing (there will likely be leftover) and garnish with cilantro or mint. Enjoy immediately with your hands, much like a taco—no forks required.

ITALIAN PUMPKIN HOLIDAY SALAD WITH GORGONZOLA AND CRANBERRY DRESSING

Cranberry dressing twinkles like tree lights, strewn across crisp romaine, roasted heirloom pumpkin, astringent yet sweet walnuts, and oily black olives for a main course (or side) fall or winter salad that, while not authentically Italian, is genuinely scrumptious. The softest gorgonzola with its robin's egg blue vein ties it all together for a rather special Big Salad.

Serves 6 as a side, 4 as a main

For the Salad

½ Italian heirloom pumpkin such as Marina Di Chioggia
   or other dry and creamy-fleshed pumpkin, halved, seeded,
   and cut into 1½–2-inch wedges

1 tablespoon extra-virgin olive oil

1 head romaine, shredded, or arugula

½ cup kalamata olives, pitted

4 ounces gorgonzola, torn into small pieces

½ cup walnuts, chopped

For the Cranberry Dressing

1 cup cranberries, fresh or frozen

¼ cup apple cider vinegar

2 tablespoons honey

¼ cup extra-virgin olive oil

¼ cup orange juice or water

½ teaspoon salt

ground black pepper, to taste

Preheat oven to 375°F. Line a large-rimmed baking sheet with parchment paper. Add pumpkin wedges to baking sheet and toss with oil. Bake for 35 to 45 minutes, until tender.

To make the dressing, in a small saucepan, combine cranberries, vinegar, and honey. Cover and bring to a simmer; reduce heat to low and cook for 5 minutes, or until cranberries burst; remove from heat. Uncover and mash cranberries with a fork; stir in olive oil, orange juice or water, salt, and pepper.

To one large platter or individual plates, add a bed of romaine followed by squash wedges, olives, and gorgonzola. Drizzle over dressing and sprinkle with walnuts. Serve immediately.

DELICATA SQUASH AND ARUGULA SALAD WITH PUMPKIN SEED OIL VINAIGRETTE

Please forget the globular, Halloween-y pumpkin for a moment, as I need to gush about my love for delicata squash: the squash with the edible skin. Tender, quick-cooking, and unquestionably good for you, delicata's butternut-sweetness tangles itself with peppery arugula and holiday-ish crunchy bits for a main course or side salad that instantly refreshes after this time of year's heavier fare. A nutty, evergreen pumpkin seed oil dressing makes this salad feel special.

.... *Serves 2–3* ....

1 (¾ pound) delicata squash, halved lengthwise, seeded, and cut into ½-inch half-moons
1 teaspoon extra-virgin olive oil
1 tablespoon pumpkin seed oil
1 tablespoon grainy mustard
1 tablespoon lemon juice
1 teaspoon maple syrup
4 cups arugula
2 heaping tablespoons dried cranberries
2 heaping tablespoons chopped pecans
¼ teaspoon salt

Preheat oven to 400°F. Line a large-rimmed baking sheet with parchment paper. Toss squash with olive oil. Roast for 20 to 25 minutes, until soft and beginning to brown on bottoms. Cool slightly.

In a large bowl, whisk together pumpkin seed oil, grainy mustard, lemon juice, and maple syrup. Add roasted squash, arugula, cranberries, pecans, and salt; gently toss to combine. Serve.

KALE SLAW WITH APPLES, WHITE CHEDDAR, AND PUMPKIN HONEY MUSTARD DRESSING

Stop right here. I know you pretended not to see this recipe, thinking, "Kale salad? Snore." Didn't you? I knew it. Yes, kale salad is good for you. Raw kale salad is even better for you. It's been done, though, many times over, and often presented in a way that feels like dietary penitence—not my style. I won't apologize for my love of vegetables, but they better taste good, dammit. Like many dark leafy greens, raw kale's bitter edge needs a bit of culinary sandpaper to even out its acerbic edges. Here, this "sandpaper" is sweet apple, pungent aged cheddar, and a honeyed pumpkin dressing.

Serves 4

For the Pumpkin Honey Mustard Dressing

¼ cup pumpkin purée

2 tablespoons extra-virgin olive oil

2 tablespoons white wine vinegar or apple cider vinegar

2 teaspoons grainy mustard

2 teaspoons honey

salt, to taste

ground black pepper, to taste

For the Kale Slaw

4 cups packed, shredded lacinato or curly kale

2 apples, any variety, cored and cut into matchsticks or thin slices

2 ounces mature (aged) white cheddar, roughly crumbled or shredded

For the dressing, whisk together all dressing ingredients in a small bowl; season with salt and pepper, to taste. Set aside.

In a large bowl, massage (squeeze) kale with hands until dark green and tender. Toss kale with apples and dressing until evenly coated; add cheddar and gently toss again. Allow slaw to sit (at room temperature or in the refrigerator) for at least 10 minutes before serving. Dressed salad will keep covered in the refrigerator for up to 2 days.

ROASTED JARRAHDALE PUMPKIN AND ONIONS WITH LEMONY WHIPPED FETA

I first had whipped feta served alongside a whole roasted cauliflower at Domenica in New Orleans, Louisiana. That appetizer was the inspiration for this recipe. Jarrahdale pumpkin, an heirloom varietal with a moss green skin and meaty tangerine interior, (becoming more and more common at supermarkets) is used here instead of cauliflower, partnered alongside glossy, balsamic-kissed onions. Cut heftily and roasted, these veggies make an ideal vehicle for the pillowy whipped feta.

.... *Serves 4* ....

For the Roasted Jarrahdale Pumpkin and Onions

½ (4–5 pound) jarrahdale pumpkin or other meaty-fleshed pumpkin, peeled, seeded, and cut into 1-inch cubes (about 2 pounds of pumpkin cubes)

2 onions, peeled and cut into 12 thick wedges

2 tablespoons balsamic vinegar

2 tablespoons extra-virgin olive oil

2 teaspoons fresh thyme, chopped, or 1 teaspoon dried thyme

½ teaspoon salt

ground black pepper, to taste

For the Lemony Whipped Feta

½ cup heavy whipping cream

4 ounces feta, roughly crumbled

¼ cup lemon juice

For Serving

½ cup chopped walnuts, raw or toasted

For the roasted pumpkin and onions, preheat oven to 375°F. On a large-rimmed baking sheet, toss all roasted pumpkin ingredients; spread in a single layer. Roast for 40 to 45 minutes, until pumpkin is tender.

For the whipped feta, in a food processor, add cream and blend until it has a bit of body. Add feta and blend until incorporated. Scrape down sides and blend. Add lemon juice and blend until incorporated. Scrape down sides and blend for 15 to 30 seconds longer, until mixture is creamy (there will still be a few small pieces of feta).

To serve, smear whipped feta on a serving plate or the interior of a bowl, top with roasted pumpkin and onions, and scatter with walnuts. Alternatively, add roasted pumpkin and onions to a serving plate or bowl, dollop over whipped feta, and scatter with walnuts. Serve warm or room temperature.

BLACK QUINOA WITH HEIRLOOM PUMPKIN, CHESTNUTS, AND MINT

As a woman who does not pride herself on being an expert gardener, I do pride myself on the ability to grow mint. In fact, I'm able to keep the tenacious herb from the first signs of spring to early November on very warm years, making it a refreshing addition to my recipes nearly yearlong. The rest of the components in this side dish are just as easygoing—something the fall and winter months aren't necessarily known for. This vibrant creation is a wholesome, speedy side to recalibrate your taste buds during the most wonderful (and hectic) time of year.

Serves 4–6

1 (2–3 pound or ½ of a large) creamy-fleshed pumpkin such as kabocha or Marina di Chioggia, halved, seeded, peeled, and cut into 1-inch cubes

1 tablespoon extra-virgin olive oil

2 cups water

1 cup uncooked black or white or red quinoa

1 cup raw almonds, roughly chopped

1 cup fresh mint, chopped, if large

16 vacuum-packed roasted chestnuts (no sugar, salt, or preservatives), roughly broken with fingers

¼ cup full-fat canned coconut milk

¼ cup lemon juice

1 tablespoon honey

½ teaspoon salt

ground black pepper, to taste

Preheat oven to 375°F. On a large-rimmed baking sheet, toss pumpkin with oil. Roast for 35 to 45 minutes, until tender and beginning to brown.

In a medium saucepan, bring water and quinoa to boil, reduce to a simmer, cover, and cook for 15 minutes. Remove from heat and steam, covered, for 5 minutes. Fluff with a fork and add to a large bowl along with roasted pumpkin.

In a medium skillet, toast almonds over medium heat until fragrant and beginning to brown (about 3 to 4 minutes). Add to quinoa and pumpkin along with mint and chestnuts.

In a small bowl, whisk coconut milk, lemon juice, honey, salt, and pepper. Add to quinoa and pumpkin mixture and toss gently to combine. Serve warm, at room temperature, or chilled.

ROASTED PUMPKIN WITH ONIONS, POMEGRANATE, AND YOGURT

To effortlessly remove the arils (pink seeds) from a pomegranate: fill a large bowl with water, quarter pomegranate, plunge each quarter into the water, and remove the arils with your fingers (they come right out—like magic). Much of the white pith floats to the top, which you can now remove, drain into a fine mesh sieve, remove any outstanding white pith, and store arils airtight in the refrigerator for 1 to 2 weeks. You can now bejewel and bedazzle all of your food with pomegranate, starting with this recipe, of course.

Serves 4

2 tablespoons extra-virgin olive oil
1 (2–3 pound) creamy-fleshed pumpkin such as red kuri or buttercup, peeled, seeded, and cut into ¼-inch wedges
1 onion, sliced into thick wedges, pieces separated
½ teaspoon salt
ground black pepper, to taste
1 cup pomegranate arils
½ cup whole milk plain yogurt (Balkan-style or Greek)

Preheat oven to 375°F. On a large-rimmed baking sheet, toss together oil, pumpkin, onion, salt, and pepper. Line in a single layer and roast for 20 to 30 minutes (depending on thickness of pumpkin wedges), until pumpkin is tender.

Spread yogurt on the bottom of a serving plate; top with roasted pumpkin and onions, and sprinkle over pomegranate. Or, place pumpkin on a serving plate, drizzle with yogurt, and top with pomegranate. Serve warm or at room temperature.

SKILLET PUMPKIN WITH BROWN BUTTER, HONEY, AND CLEMENTINE

Browning butter will take an additional minute to this 10(ish)-minute side, but I assure you it's worth it. Festive, sticky, and seriously addictive, this squashy skillet side delivers a bit of elegance to your everyday dinner plate.

.... *Serves 4* ....

3 tablespoons salted butter
1 (2–3 pound) creamy-fleshed pumpkin such as buttercup,
    peeled, seeded, and cut into ½-inch cubes
2 tablespoons clementine juice (from 1 clementine) or orange juice
1 tablespoon honey
¼ teaspoon salt
ground black pepper, to taste

In a large high-sided skillet, melt butter over medium heat. Continue to cook over medium until a light brown color (2 to 3 minutes). Immediately transfer to a bowl (including brown bits). To brown butter (keep it in the bowl, the fat will splash and burn you if you leave the brown butter in the pan), stir in clementine or orange juice and honey. Add back to skillet along with pumpkin and salt. Mix to combine and return skillet to element; increase heat to medium-high and cook until mixture bubbles. Reduce to a simmer, cover, and cook for 10 minutes. Uncover and cook until sauce has thickened (about 2 minutes). Sprinkle with black pepper and serve immediately.

MILLET COUSCOUS WITH ROASTED PARSNIPS, PUMPKIN, AND MINT

Millet is a gluten-free, BB-esque whole grain that acts in lieu of couscous (a small pasta made from wheat) in this North African–inspired side. Parsnips contribute an inherently cinnamon-spiced taste and meaty texture, balancing cubes of creamy pumpkin and refreshing mint.

.... *Serves 4–6* ....

1 (2–3 pound) creamy-fleshed pumpkin such as red kuri or butternut, peeled, seeded, and cut into ½-inch cubes

2 parsnips, peeled and cut into 1-inch matchsticks

2 tablespoons refined avocado oil or extra-virgin olive oil

½ teaspoon salt, plus more to taste

ground black pepper, to taste

⅔ cup millet

1⅓ cups low-sodium vegetable stock or water

1 cup fresh mint, finely chopped

2 tablespoons lemon juice

2 teaspoons ground cumin

Preheat oven to 425°F. On a large-rimmed baking sheet, toss pumpkin, parsnips, oil, salt, and pepper. Roast for 30 to 35 minutes, until tender and beginning to brown. Transfer to a large mixing bowl.

While vegetables are roasting, bring millet and stock or water to a boil, reduce to simmer, cover, and cook for 20 minutes. Remove from heat and steam, covered, for 5 minutes. Fluff with a fork and add to bowl with roasted vegetables along with mint, lemon juice, and cumin; toss to combine, season with additional salt, if desired, and serve warm or room temperature.

WARM WILD RICE WITH SPINACH, PUMPKIN, AND GRAPES

In my first cookbook, *Whole Bowls*, I created a dish similar to this one, inspired by the wine country a couple hours from my home. I topped that recipe with halloumi, a salty, squeaky cheese, which I could see working here as well if you cubed it up for griddling instead of one big slab, but goat cheese or feta would also do well with these flavors.

·· *Serves 8* ··

4 cups water

1 cup uncooked wild rice

1 (2–3 pound or ½ of a large) creamy-fleshed pumpkin such as jarrahdale, halved, seeded, peeled, and cut into 1-inch cubes

5 tablespoons extra-virgin olive oil, divided

8 ounces (6 cups packed) pre-washed baby spinach

2 cups (14 ounces) halved seedless red or green grapes

2 tablespoons balsamic vinegar

1 teaspoon salt

ground black pepper, to taste

Preheat oven to 375ºF. In a medium saucepan, bring water and rice to a boil, reduce to medium-low heat, partially cover, and cook for 40 to 50 minutes, until grains are burst and rice is tender. Drain, add back to pot, cover, and keep warm with the residual heat of the stove element. While rice is cooking, roast the pumpkin.

On a large-rimmed baking sheet, toss pumpkin with 1 tablespoon oil. Roast in preheated oven for 35 to 45 minutes, until tender and beginning to brown. Add to a large bowl along with rice, spinach, grapes, remaining 4 tablespoons oil, vinegar, salt, and pepper. Gently toss until combined, allowing to warm squash and rice to slightly wilt the spinach. Transfer to a serving dish and serve warm or at room temperature.

VANILLA ROASTED PUMPKIN WEDGES

To enhance pumpkin's inherent vanilla essence, vanilla extract is added (which doesn't make this taste like dessert, I promise), teasing out those gorgeous, heady floral notes. If you're using a pumpkin with small, tender seeds, they can be roasted along with the pumpkin flesh, adding a bit of rustic charm and meatiness.

Serves 4–6

1 regular or ½ large (2–3 pounds) creamy-fleshed pumpkin such as cinderella or butternut, halved, seeded (seeds reserved, if desired), and cut into 1-inch wedges
1 tablespoon extra-virgin olive oil
1 tablespoon white wine vinegar or orange juice
½ teaspoon vanilla extract or paste or fresh vanilla bean seeds
¼ teaspoon cinnamon
¼ teaspoon salt
ground black pepper, to taste

Preheat oven to 400ºF. On a large-rimmed baking sheet lined with parchment paper, combine all ingredients including reserved pumpkin seeds, if using. Roast for 40 to 50 minutes, until tender and beginning to caramelize. Serve warm.

TWICE-BAKED MASHED PUMPKIN AND APPLES WITH PECAN OAT CRUNCH

As a Canadian, the traditional sweet potato casserole topped with marshmallows served on American Thanksgiving (Canada has Thanksgiving early October) perplexed me for years. It seemed strange, a side dish with that much saccharinity, but here I am, eating my words, giving you a sweet side (naturally so, with no added sugar) I've gladly eaten for breakfast with tangy plain yogurt and dessert with vanilla ice cream. Alas, I'm still waiting for my invitation to the grand American Thanksgiving table to heap my plate full of the marshmallow stuff (hint, hint, American readers) —I'll bring this along to share.

.... *Serves 4* ....

1 (2–3 pound) creamy-fleshed pumpkin such as buttercup, halved, and seeded

2 cups (2–3 regular) shredded apple, any variety

¼ cup full-fat canned coconut milk or heavy whipping cream

1 teaspoon salt

⅛ teaspoon ground cloves

Pecan Oat Crunch

¼ cup unsalted butter, melted

½ cup chopped pecans

½ cup large-flake rolled oats (not instant)

½ teaspoon salt

Preheat oven to 375°F. Line a large-rimmed baking sheet with parchment paper and place pumpkin cut-side down (skin faces up). Roast for 45 to 60 minutes, until collapsed and extremely tender when pierced with a knife. Cool until you can handle it comfortably.

To purée, scoop cooled pumpkin flesh into a food processor; discard skin. Blend until smooth and creamy, stopping to scrape down sides once or twice. Measure out 2 cups pumpkin purée and add to a large bowl with apples, coconut milk or cream, salt, and cloves. Spread evenly into a 9-inch ceramic or glass pie dish, or 8 x 8–inch ceramic or glass dish, or medium-sized individual ramekins.

In a medium bowl, mix all ingredients for topping and evenly distribute over pumpkin mixture. Bake for 40 to 45 minutes, until bubbling around the edges and topping begins to brown. Serve warm.

LEMONY ROASTED BRUSSELS SPROUTS AND PUMPKIN SEEDS

Every food writer says the same thing when discussing Brussels sprouts: "I grew up with steamed/boiled Brussels sprouts, which made me hate them—then I discovered *roasted* Brussels sprouts and it changed my life!" Sure, roasted Brussels sprouts are the best way to eat these adorable baby cabbages, but I'd eat a steamed/boiled Brussels sprout just the same; I love them that much. To keep up with the Joneses, I've roasted the sprouts for this recipe, their burnished exterior and meltingly tender interior contrasting beautifully with crispy, popped pumpkin seeds. The lemon (which you eat in its entirety, including the peel) is also roasted because roasting citrus changed my life!

....   *Serves 4*   ....

1 pound Brussels sprouts, tough ends removed, halved lengthwise

½ whole lemon, thinly sliced into rounds, seeds removed

¼ cup raw, unsalted green pumpkin seeds

1 tablespoon extra-virgin olive oil

½ teaspoon salt

Preheat oven to 400°F.

On a large-rimmed baking sheet, toss together all ingredients and spread into a single layer with sprouts cut-side down. Roast for 15 to 20 minutes, until tender and sprouts are beginning to brown on bottoms. Serve, and don't forget you are able to eat the whole lemon when roasted, peel and all.

WHOLE ROASTED CINDERELLA PUMPKIN

Kitschy and whimsical—akin to the holiday season itself.

·· *Serves 10–12* ··

1 (6–7 pound) cinderella pumpkin

Preheat oven to 350ºF. Line a large-rimmed baking sheet with foil or parchment paper.

Using a very sharp paring knife, score a circle around the top of the pumpkin, leaving 2 to 3 inches between the stem and perimeter. In a small incision, cut the top off (much like you do for carving a jack-o'-lantern); slice off any seeds or stringy bit on the top piece; set aside. Scoop out pumpkin seeds and any overly stringy flesh. Place pumpkin, hole-side up on prepared baking sheet and with its top, stem-side up. Bake for 1 to 1½ hours, until tender and beginning to collapse.

To serve, place on a large platter, pop on the top, and slice into wedges with a serrated knife. Serve with salt and butter.

MAINS

Finally, after the drinks and apps and preparations, it's time to set the table for dinner. I eat very well, and because of my job, I eat a lot, especially at dinner, which is why the majority of these recipes verge on the healthy, feel-good side, as opposed to the overly decadent, rich side; so, you'll notice a fair amount of produce in these recipes (besides pumpkin), as well as the use of whole grains, alternative proteins, and healthy fats. Cooking with whole foods is something more of us are warming up to, and a way I've enjoyed cooking and eating since my early twenties. Saying this, I assure you these feel-good recipes will make your taste buds feel good, too—in fact, I promise you.

For the twenty-minute cooks and the unhurried bunch. For weeknights and weekends. For casual parties and elegant gatherings. For school nights and work nights and movie nights and date nights. For every single holiday during the endless holidays. Any pumpkin lover (or convert a pumpkin disbeliever) should be able to find a recipe for dinner tonight.

RECITES

PIZZA WITH PUMPKIN, GOAT CHEESE, AND KALE

159

CORNUCOPIA-STUFFED PUMPKIN

160

APPLE AND CHEESE MELTS WITH PUMPKIN KETCHUP

162

GRAIN BOWLS WITH APPLE CIDER VINEGAR–ROASTED PUMPKIN AND KIMCHI

164

BEAN AND RED LENTIL PUMPKIN CHILI WITH ZUCCHINI

167

WILD MUSHROOM AND PUMPKIN BARLEY RISOTTO

168

PUMPKIN VEGGIE BURGERS WITH HALLOUMI AND AVOCADO

171

BLACK PASTA WITH ROASTED PUMPKIN AND CHILI

173

RAPINI AND ROASTED GARLIC PUMPKIN GALETTE WITH ROSEMARY SPELT CRUST

174

MELLOW MEYER LEMON PUMPKIN CURRY BOWLS

177

HEIRLOOM PUMPKIN GNOCCHI WITH MINT AND GARLIC

179

HEIRLOOM PUMPKIN GNOCCHI WITH OVEN-ROASTED TOMATO SAUCE

180

SILKY PUMPKIN PASTA WITH ROASTED BRUSSELS SPROUTS AND
CRISPY LEAVES

183

MOROCCAN CHICKPEA, PUMPKIN, AND PRUNE STEW

184

MUSHROOMS AND KALE OVER PUMPKIN POLENTA

187

FIRECRACKER STIR-FRIED PUMPKIN, BOK CHOY, AND CASHEWS

188

SOCCA PIZZA WITH ROASTED SQUASH, BRUSSELS SPROUTS,
AND LEMON

191

LASAGNA WITH PUMPKIN ORANGE BÉCHAMEL AND RICOTTA
PARMESAN BÉCHAMEL

192

VEGAN PUMPKIN, ONION, AND SPINACH LASAGNA WITH WHITE BEAN
RICOTTA

195

CURRIED PUMPKIN TOFU CALZONES

196

PIZZA WITH PUMPKIN, GOAT CHEESE, AND KALE

Pizza is one of my all-time favorite foods—completely unoriginal, maybe, but I'm okay with that. And, the sky is the limit with toppings when it comes to this beloved staple. A crisp, nutty, spelt thin-crust is employed as a blank slate, eager to take on the warming, cool weather ingredients of pumpkin and kale. It's all tied together with snowballs of goat cheese (though you could use fresh mozzarella, blue cheese, brie, or feta if you prefer) for a slice of the good stuff, entirely transformed from its tomato-sauce roots.

.... *Serves 8* ....

For the Spelt Pizza Dough

2 cups lukewarm water

2 tablespoons quick-rise yeast (about 3 packages minus ¼ teaspoon)

2 tablespoons granulated sugar

1 tablespoon extra-virgin olive oil, plus more for bowl

4 cups light or dark spelt flour

2 teaspoons salt

For the Pizza

1 (2–3 pound) creamy-fleshed pumpkin such as red kuri or butternut, seeded, peeled, and cut into ½-inch cubes or wedges

1 tablespoon extra-virgin olive oil, plus more for brushing

salt, to taste

½ bunch lacinato kale, de-stemmed and roughly torn

8 ounces goat cheese

For the dough, mix water, yeast, and sugar together. Set aside to proof for 10 minutes, until foamy. Stir in olive oil. In a stand mixer fitted with a dough hook, or by hand, mix together flour and salt. With machine running on low, or stirring by hand, slowly mix in yeast mixture. Knead in machine or by hand until elastic (about 3 minutes by machine and 8 minutes by hand). Coat a large bowl with oil, add dough, cover with a kitchen towel, and set aside to rise for 2 hours or refrigerate overnight, bringing to room temperature before rolling.

To cook the pumpkin, preheat oven to 375°F. On a large-rimmed baking sheet, toss pumpkin with oil and salt, to taste. Roast for 30 to 35 minutes until tender. Cool slightly.

Turn oven heat up to 425°F.

Punch down dough and cut into 8 pieces. Generously flour your counter and dust a bit on a large-rimmed baking sheet. Roll each of the 8 pieces into very thin (about ¼- to ⅛-inch) pieces. Place on baking sheet; each baking sheet will fit 2 personal-sized pizzas. Brush dough with olive oil. Top pizza with a scattering of squash (don't overdo it!), kale, and goat cheese. Bake for 20 to 25 minutes until dough is crispy. Slice and serve immediately. Repeat with remaining dough and pizza toppings.

> **NOTES**
>
> The pizza dough can be frozen (either as 1 large or 8 small pieces), wrapped in plastic, and stored in a freezer bag for up to 6 months. Defrost and bring to room temperature before rolling.

CORNUCOPIA-STUFFED PUMPKIN

The ultimate holiday centerpiece, this whole roasted pumpkin is bursting with a rich, umami quinoa and wild mushroom stuffing with a few dried cranberry sparkles to sweeten the deal. There are many steps involved for the filling, albeit, not hard ones; however, you can make it ahead and all that's left to do the day-of is stuff and bake. If you want to get all ceremonial about this pumpkin as you would a turkey, carve (slicing into wedges) standing at the end of your harvest table a la Norman Rockwell's iconic Thanksgiving portrait—though I'd skip that tragic frilly apron.

Serves 6–8

1½ cups water
⅔ cup white quinoa
½ cup black quinoa
2 large eggs
½ cup fresh parsley, chopped
½ cup dried cranberries, chopped

2 tablespoons white wine vinegar
2 ounces (2 heaping cups) mixed wild mushrooms
1½ cups recently boiled water
¼ cup unsalted butter
1 onion, finely chopped
3 cloves garlic, minced

1 tablespoon dried sage
1 tablespoon dried thyme
1 tablespoon salt
ground black pepper, to taste
1 (6–7 pound) flat white boer pumpkin or cinderella pumpkin

Preheat oven to 350°F. Line a large-rimmed baking sheet with foil.

In a medium saucepan, bring water and white and black quinoas to a boil, reduce to a simmer, cover, and cook for 15 minutes. Remove from heat and steam, covered, for 5 minutes. Fluff with a fork and transfer to a large mixing bowl to cool slightly (as not to cook the eggs). Stir in eggs, parsley, cranberries, and vinegar.

Add dried mushrooms to a large bowl and cover with recently boiled water. Let stand for 15 minutes. Tear any large pieces and remove any tough stems. Add mushrooms and soaking water to quinoa; mix to combine.

In a large high-sided skillet, melt butter over medium heat. Add onion, garlic, sage, thyme, salt, and pepper; reduce heat to medium-low and sauté for 8 to 10 minutes, until vegetables are soft. Set aside to cool slightly. Stir into quinoa mixture.

Using a very sharp paring knife, score a circle around the top of the pumpkin, leaving 2 to 3 inches between the stem and perimeter. With a small incision, cut the top off (much like you do for carving a jack-o'-lantern); slice off any seeds or stringy bit on the top piece; set aside. Scoop out pumpkin seeds and any overly stringy flesh. Place two large pieces of foil in a cross on prepared, foil-lined baking sheet; place pumpkin in the center of the cross, hole-side up. Pack interior of pumpkin with stuffing, close foil to completely encase the pumpkin; cut another piece of foil to cover the top, if necessary. Place the top, stem-side up, next to the pumpkin.

Roast pumpkin for 1 hour; remove stem and set aside. Continue to roast for approximately 2 hours longer, until pumpkin is tender and stuffing is cooked. Remove from oven and let rest for 10 minutes. Slice into wedges with a serrated knife. Serve hot.

APPLE AND CHEESE MELTS WITH PUMPKIN KETCHUP

For me, anything even remotely resembling a grilled cheese had better come with a condiment, preferably ketchup, and this thick, rich, no-cook pumpkin variation is just what the cheesy sandwich doctor ordered. For a weekend lunch or late dinner in front of the television, I can't think of a better meal to devour on a blustery evening at home.

Serves 4, with extra Pumpkin Ketchup

For the Pumpkin Ketchup

2 cups pumpkin purée

1⅓ cups tomato paste

1 cup distilled white vinegar

¼ cup honey

¼ cup dehydrated chopped onions

2 teaspoons salt

1 teaspoon granulated dried garlic (not garlic salt)

1 teaspoon ground cloves

For the Apple and Cheese Melts

4 thick slices grainy sourdough bread

8 ounces cheese, any variety (cheddar, gorgonzola, brie, mozzarella, etc.)

2 apples, any variety, halved, cored, and very thinly sliced

fresh herbs of choice (rosemary, thyme, basil, chives, etc.)

For the ketchup, in a large bowl, whisk all ketchup ingredients until combined. Store in refrigerator for up to 1 month or freeze for up to 3 months.

For the melts, place oven rack in the center position. Preheat broiler low. Add bread to a large-rimmed baking sheet, top with apple slices, cheese, and a few sprigs of fresh herbs. Broil for about 5 minutes, or until cheese is bubbling and beginning to brown. Slice in half (optional) and serve immediately with ketchup.

NOTES

Instead of apples, try ripe pears.

GRAIN BOWLS WITH APPLE CIDER VINEGAR–ROASTED PUMPKIN AND KIMCHI

A nod to my first cookbook, *Whole Bowls*, this trendy, plant-based, complete meal has an unexpected sharpness from the vinegary roasted pumpkin and, of course, a very expected sharpness from the five-alarm kimchi. Make this meal your own by mixing and matching the components to suit your tastes.

.... *Serves 4* ....

Apple Cider Vinegar–Roasted Pumpkin

½ (2–3 pound) creamy-fleshed pumpkin such as kabocha, seeded, peeled, and cut into ½-inch cubes

¼ cup apple cider vinegar

1 tablespoon coconut oil

1 tablespoon tamari

Protein Suggestions (choose one or more)

silken tofu, cubed

fried eggs

cooked white beans

For Assembly

2–3 cups cooked brown rice or grain of choice, warm

1 cup prepared kimchi (I get mine from a Korean restaurant in my city)

For the pumpkin, preheat oven to 400°F. Line a large-rimmed baking sheet with parchment paper; add squash. In a small saucepan over medium-low, heat vinegar, coconut oil, and tamari until coconut oil is melted; add to squash, toss, and roast for 35 to 40 minutes, until tender and beginning to caramelize. To serve, add prepared components. Serve warm, at room temperature, or chilled.

BEAN AND RED LENTIL PUMPKIN CHILI WITH ZUCCHINI

If I watched football, I would make this chili to feast on during the game. Alas, like many sports, the rules of football elude me, so making a bowl of this hearty bean dish pair a touch better with reruns of *Buffy*—for me, at least.

Serves 6

2 tablespoons refined avocado oil or extra-virgin olive oil

1 onion, diced

1 large or 2 small zucchinis, cut into ½-inch pieces

4 cloves garlic, minced

1 tablespoon ground cumin

1 teaspoon smoked paprika or chili powder

½ teaspoon chili flakes

½ teaspoon dried oregano

1 (28-ounce) can whole or diced tomatoes

1½ cups pumpkin purée

1½ cups water

¼ cup apple cider vinegar

1 (19-ounce) can black beans or 2 cups cooked black beans, drained and rinsed if using canned

1 cup uncooked red lentils

1 teaspoon salt, plus more to taste

pea sprouts, for serving

corn tortilla wedges or chips, for serving

In a large pot, warm oil over medium heat. Add onion, zucchini, garlic, cumin, smoked paprika or chili powder, chili flakes, and oregano; sauté for 8 to 10 minutes, until vegetables are soft and beginning to brown. Stir in tomatoes, pumpkin, water, and vinegar, followed by black beans, red lentils, and salt. Bring to a boil, reduce to a simmer, cover, and cook, stirring a few times, for 30 to 40 minutes, until lentils are tender. Season with additional salt, if desired. Ladle into bowls, garnish with pea sprouts and tortillas, and serve.

WILD MUSHROOM AND PUMPKIN BARLEY RISOTTO

The traditional risotto grain, Arborio rice, is replaced with chewy, nutty barley, a whole grain with bite. Earthy wild mushrooms lend meatiness and umami-packed flavor to this special occasion–seeming entrée, while pumpkin purée works to create a gorgeously rich, thick gravy with the mushroom "broth" (made from rehydrating the dried wild mushrooms).

Serves 4–5

3 ounces (85 grams) dried mixed wild
   mushrooms
2 cups hot tap water
2 tablespoons unsalted butter
1 onion, diced
2 cloves garlic, minced
½ teaspoon dried sage
½ teaspoon dried thyme

½ teaspoon salt, plus more to taste
ground black pepper, to taste
¾ cup pearl barley
2½ cups low-sodium vegetable stock
1 cup pumpkin purée (I like to use earthy
   kabocha for this, but canned is also excellent)
1 tablespoon white wine vinegar

Add mushrooms to a large bowl and cover with hot tap water. Rehydrate for 15 minutes while you prepare the risotto. Do not discard liquid since you'll use it all (this is the mushroom "broth").

In a large high-sided skillet or pot, heat butter over medium. Add onion, garlic, sage, thyme, salt, and pepper. Reduce heat to medium-low; sauté for 8 to 10 minutes, until soft. Add barley, increase heat to medium, and toast for 1 minute. Stir in stock, pumpkin, mushrooms including rehydrating water, and vinegar. Bring to a boil, reduce to a simmer, and cook over low, stirring often, for 20 minutes. Cover and continue to cook over low, stirring often, for 30 minutes longer. Taste to make sure barley is tender and there's enough salt to your liking. Serve immediately.

PUMPKIN VEGGIE BURGERS WITH HALLOUMI AND AVOCADO

I'm going to play favorites: I have a bit of a thing for this recipe. When you get the perfect bite of super-savory pumpkin burger, squeaky halloumi, buttery avocado, crisp greens, and quality bread, you may need to take a moment to collect your thoughts. And there's no need to freeze your buns off outside at the grill to experience this phenomenon—it's a stovetop and oven-only meal.

Makes 7 burgers

For the Pumpkin Veggie Burgers

1 (19-ounce) can chickpeas or 2 cups cooked chickpeas, drained and rinsed if using canned

1 cup pumpkin purée, preferably canned or from a dry-fleshed pumpkin such as kabocha (see *Notes*)

¾ cup quick-cooking rolled oats

½ cup fresh cilantro or fresh parsley, roughly chopped

1 large egg

1 clove garlic, minced

1 tablespoon extra-virgin olive oil

1 tablespoon lemon juice, plus more for serving

1 tablespoon dried chopped onion

1¼ teaspoon salt (you can cut it back to 1 teaspoon if using canned beans with added salt)

ground black pepper, to taste

For Serving

sourdough bread or burger buns of choice, toasted or untoasted

1 (8-ounce) package halloumi (halloom), sliced into ¼-inch slabs

avocado, sliced

leaf lettuce or de-stemmed lacinato kale

For the burgers, preheat oven to 425°F and line a large-rimmed baking sheet with parchment paper. In a large bowl, roughly mash chickpeas with the back of a fork until most are mashed, leaving some whole. Mix in remaining burger ingredients. Set aside for 15 minutes. After resting, scoop ½-cup portions onto prepared baking sheet, forming into patties ½-inch high. Bake for 15 minutes, carefully flip, and bake for 5 minutes longer.

For serving, preheat a large nonstick skillet to medium-high. Add halloumi in a single layer and cook until bottom is golden brown (1 to 2 minutes), flip and cook for 30 seconds longer. Assemble burgers on bread or buns with lettuce or kale, a fan of avocado (or mash it into the bread first), veggie burger, and a couple slices of halloumi, squeeze with lemon, and top with another piece of bread or bun, if desired. Serve warm.

BLACK PASTA WITH ROASTED PUMPKIN AND CHILI

Black pasta is simply white pasta wearing a flawlessly tailored tuxedo, looking and feeling special occasion appropriate (and a touch scary). Halloween's orange and black color palette was the inspiration behind this unique meal, as were the bright, full-bodied tastes of Asian cuisine's lip-smacking noodle dishes. The black-tie pasta is tangled with vibrant pieces of roasted pumpkin, topped with a sunshine-yellow egg yolk (which "cooks" in the bowl, creating a slick sauce), and gets perked up with fiery chili, making for a spookily delicious dinner to enjoy during the witching season.

Serves 4

½ (2–3 pound) creamy-fleshed pumpkin such as red kuri or butternut, seeded, peeled, and cut into ½-inch cubes

4 tablespoons extra-virgin olive oil, divided

salt, to taste

¾ pound (12 ounces) black spaghetti or spaghetti of choice

½ cup reserved pasta cooking liquid

1–2 red chilis, seeded and minced (use the full amount for a spicier dish)

2 cloves garlic, minced

1 tablespoon honey

4 egg yolks, kept whole (look for very fresh, local eggs, if possible)

Preheat oven to 375°F. On a large-rimmed baking sheet, toss pumpkin with 1 tablespoon oil and salt to taste. Roast for 30 to 35 minutes until tender. Set aside.

Bring a large pot of water to a boil; salt well. Cook pasta according to package directions (about 8 minutes for al dente). Reserve ½ cup pasta water. Drain pasta.

To the pasta cooking pot, heat remaining 3 tablespoons oil over medium heat. Add garlic, chili, and honey; cook for 30 seconds to 1 minute. Add drained pasta and roasted squash, loosening with reserved water if necessary; toss until heated through. Serve, garnishing each bowl of pasta with 1 egg yolk. (This creates a creamy sauce and "cooks" when tossed into the hot pasta.)

RAPINI AND ROASTED GARLIC PUMPKIN GALETTE WITH ROSEMARY SPELT CRUST

Galettes thrive on imperfection—the more rustic in appearance, the better. Encased in a ragged herbed spelt pastry is a base of roasted garlic–infused pumpkin and bitter, forest green rapini. I like to serve this as a vegetarian main course for Thanksgiving, but it would work equally well as a side dish for meat-eaters at your gathering.

Serves 4 as a main, 6 as a side

1 head garlic, halved horizontally

1 cup pumpkin purée

2 teaspoons white wine vinegar

1¼ teaspoons salt, divided

ground black pepper, to taste

1 bunch rapini (broccoli rabe), tough ends removed, roughly chopped

2 teaspoons extra-virgin olive oil

½ recipe Spelt Pie Crust (see page **244**)

dark or light spelt flour, for rolling

1 tablespoon fresh rosemary, dried or chopped

¼ teaspoon ground nutmeg

1 tablespoon heavy cream

Preheat oven to 400°F. Wrap head of garlic in a tight ball of foil or parchment paper, place on a baking sheet, and roast for 45 minutes, until soft. Reserve half and save the remaining for another recipe (store leftovers covered in the refrigerator). Thoroughly mash and mix garlic with pumpkin, vinegar, 1 teaspoon salt, and pepper. Cover and refrigerate until ready to assemble (or overnight).

In a large high-sided skillet, steam rapini with a splash of water until tender and dark green. Drain any excess water, return to pot, and mix in olive oil and remaining ¼ teaspoon salt. Cool until rapini is room temperature (or cover and refrigerate overnight).

Lightly flour counter and a rolling pin. Sprinkle crust dough with rosemary and nutmeg (it will incorporate as you roll), and roll into a rough circle until ¼ inch in thickness, moving dough and adding more flour as necessary to prevent sticking. Transfer to a large-rimmed baking sheet.

Spread bottom of dough with pumpkin mixture, leaving a 2-inch border around the perimeter. Mound cooled rapini on top of pumpkin. Fold edges of galette up to encase the filling, overlapping as you form a rough circle. Brush exposed dough with cream.

Bake in a 400°F oven for 20 minutes. Increase heat to 425°F and bake for 15 to 20 minutes longer, until crust is golden brown and crispy. Cool for a few minutes before slicing and serving. This tastes delicious warm or at room temperature.

MELLOW MEYER LEMON PUMPKIN CURRY BOWLS

The produce that comes into season during the same time of year informs my cooking tremendously—what grows together, goes together. Meyer lemons make a brief appearance during the winter when the very last of the fresh pumpkin and squash are hanging on. This sunshine-imbued fruit is a much sweeter variety of lemon, with a fully edible skin and gorgeous aroma; it's a natural pairing for a wintery, weeknight curry bowl (though leftovers the following few days may be my favorite part about it).

Serves 4

2 tablespoons extra-virgin olive oil or coconut oil

½ (2–3 pound) creamy-fleshed pumpkin such as red kuri or butternut, seeded, peeled, and cut into ½-inch cubes

1 onion, sliced

2 cloves garlic, minced

2 teaspoons milk curry powder

½ teaspoon garam masala

½ teaspoon ground turmeric

1 (19-ounce) can chickpeas or 2 cups cooked chickpeas, drained and rinsed if using canned

¾ cup water

¼ cup meyer lemon juice

zest of 1 meyer lemon

1 teaspoon salt

ground black pepper, to taste

cooked quinoa, for serving

steamed spinach, for serving

1 meyer lemon, thinly sliced and seeded, for serving

In a large pot, heat oil over medium. Add pumpkin or squash, onion, garlic, curry, garam masala, and turmeric; sauté for 10 minutes, until vegetables begin to soften. Stir in chickpeas, water, lemon juice and zest, salt, and pepper. Bring to a boil, reduce to a simmer, cover, and cook, stirring once or twice, for 15 to 20 minutes, until vegetables are very soft. To serve, add curry to bowls along with cooked quinoa and steamed spinach, garnish with lemon slices. Serve immediately.

HEIRLOOM PUMPKIN GNOCCHI WITH MINT AND GARLIC

For this recipe, I prefer the Italian heirloom pumpkin, Marina Di Chioggia, bred specifically for gnocchi making. Try this recipe with mint and garlic for something fresh, or flip to the saucier oven-roasted tomato version on the following page.

Serves 5–6

1 Italian heirloom pumpkin such as Marina Di Chioggia, halved, and seeded, or 1 cup pumpkin purée
½ cup full-fat plain Greek yogurt
½ teaspoon salt

2 cups whole wheat pastry flour, plus more as needed
¼ cup extra-virgin olive oil, plus more for serving
2 cloves garlic, minced
1 cup fresh mint, roughly chopped if large
lemon wedges, for serving

Preheat oven to 375°F. Line a large-rimmed baking sheet with parchment paper and place pumpkin cut-side down (skin faces up). Roast for 55 to 70 minutes, until extremely tender when pierced with a knife. Cool until you can handle it comfortably.

To purée, scoop cooled pumpkin flesh into a food processor; discard skin. Blend until smooth and creamy, stopping to scrape down sides once or twice. Measure 1 cup purée and add to a large bowl. Store extra purée in a zip-top bag in the freezer for up to four months for use in any recipe calling for pumpkin purée.

To pumpkin purée, mix in yogurt and salt. Using a wooden spoon, gradually stir in flour (you may need more, depending on the water content of your pumpkin), using your hands to knead until a dough forms (looks like pizza dough at this point). Divide dough into 4 pieces. Wash and dry hands.

Line a large-rimmed baking sheet with parchment paper. On a lightly floured clean counter, roll dough portions into a ½-inch wide rope. Cut rope into ½-inch pieces with a sharp knife and transfer to prepared baking sheet. Using your finger, create a gentle indent in each gnocchi (like a belly button). Repeat with remaining dough.

At this point, gnocchi can be individually frozen on baking sheet until solid (about 2 hours) and transferred to a zip-top bag. Boil directly from freezer according to cooking directions below, making sure water remains boiling (you may need to cook for an additional minute).

To cook gnocchi, bring a large pot of water to a boil; salt well. Boil gnocchi for 4 to 6 minutes, or until they've floated to the top and are heated through. Drain well.

To the same large pot (drained), add olive oil and garlic. Briefly heat over medium until garlic is fragrant. Stir in cooked gnocchi and mint, gently tossing to coat until heated through. Serve immediately with olive oil and lemon wedges.

HEIRLOOM PUMPKIN GNOCCHI WITH OVEN-ROASTED TOMATO SAUCE

For a makeover of the previous recipe's gnocchi dish, I employ one of my back-pocket pantry sauces. Oven roasting instills canned tomatoes with a cooked-all-day richness, and it's a bit easier than any stovetop version, as pot stirring is not required. You can easily halve this sauce recipe, but I always make it in this quantity to freeze for a rainy day for use as a pizza sauce, pasta sauce, dipping sauce, and soup base. A bright shaved fennel or green salad is all you need to round out this meal.

Serves 6, with extra Oven-Roasted Tomato Sauce

2 (28-ounce) cans whole tomatoes

2 onions, roughly chopped

5 cloves garlic, roughly chopped

¼ cup extra-virgin olive oil

¼ cup red wine

2 teaspoons salt (use slightly less if your canned tomatoes have salt added)

1 recipe Heirloom Pumpkin Gnocchi (see page **179**)

Preheat oven to 375°F. To a large-rimmed baking sheet (or two smaller, large-rimmed baking sheets), add tomatoes, onions, garlic, olive oil, wine, and salt. Crush tomatoes with your hands and mix all ingredients until incorporated. Roast for 1 to 1¼ hours, until bubbling and thick. Cool for 30 minutes. Add to a food processor or blender and pulse until coarsely chopped (leave some texture). Reserve half of the sauce for use in this recipe and freeze remaining half for up to 2 months.

To cook gnocchi, bring a large pot of water to a boil; salt well. Boil gnocchi for 4 to 6 minutes, or until they've floated to the top and are heated through. Drain well. Transfer back to the same large pot along with half of prepared sauce. Cook over medium heat, stirring often, until heated through (about 2 minutes). Serve immediately.

SILKY PUMPKIN PASTA WITH ROASTED BRUSSELS SPROUTS AND CRISPY LEAVES

Mimicking a silky, smooth, slightly smoky pasta carbonara, pumpkin purée does a bit of magicking, turning this main into a produce-packed, vegan alternative. Use whatever shape of pasta you enjoy or have handy, from spaghetti to linguini to penne to rigatoni—the sauce will work in any arena.

·· *Serves 4* ··

1 pound Brussels sprouts, tough ends removed, halved

¼ cup plus 2 teaspoons extra-virgin olive oil, divided

8 ounces whole grain spaghetti or pasta of choice

1 cup reserved pasta cooking liquid

3 cloves garlic, minced

1 teaspoon dried thyme

½ teaspoon smoked paprika

¼ teaspoon nutmeg

1 cup pumpkin purée

1½ tablespoons lemon juice

1 teaspoon salt

ground black pepper, to taste

Preheat oven to 375ºF. Bring a bring a large pot of water to a boil; salt well.

On a large-rimmed baking sheet, toss Brussels sprouts with 2 teaspoons oil, separating some of the outer leaves to get crispy. Roast for 15 to 20 minutes until tender and beginning to brown.

Meanwhile, cook pasta according to package directions (about 8 minutes for al dente). Reserve 1 cup cooking liquid. Drain.

In a large high-sided skillet, heat remaining ¼ cup oil over medium. Add garlic, thyme, smoked paprika, and nutmeg; sauté for 1 to 2 minutes, until fragrant. Stir in pumpkin, lemon juice, salt, pepper, and reserved pasta cooking liquid. Add pasta and half of roasted Brussels sprouts; toss until heated through

To serve, add pasta to bowls and top with remaining roasted Brussels sprouts, making sure to include some of the crispy, charred leaves. Serve immediately.

MOROCCAN CHICKPEA, PUMPKIN, AND PRUNE STEW

The heady aromas of the spice route perfume this deeply satisfying tagine. Rice or couscous are an idyllic side, their blandness playing off the assertive flavors found in each bite. It's versatile, too. For instance, prunes can be changed for dried apricots; for meat eaters, substitute the chickpeas with chicken; and your garnishes can range from yogurt to cilantro to chopped toasted almonds.

Serves 4

2 tablespoons extra-virgin olive oil

1 onion, thinly sliced

3 cloves garlic, minced

1 (19-ounce) can chickpeas or 2 cups cooked chickpeas, drained and rinsed if using canned

2 cups peeled and seeded cubed pumpkin, any variety, cut into 1-inch pieces

1 cup water

¾ cup pitted prunes (dried plums), halved

1 tablespoon apple cider vinegar or lemon juice

1 teaspoon salt

1 teaspoon ground cumin

½ teaspoon ground cinnamon

¼ teaspoon chili flakes

¼ teaspoon saffron

ground black pepper, to taste

warm rice or couscous, for serving (optional)

In a large high-sided skillet or pot, heat oil over medium. Add onion and garlic; sauté for 8 to 10 minutes, until soft and beginning to brown. Mix in chickpeas, pumpkin, water, prunes, vinegar or lemon juice, salt, cumin, cinnamon, chili, saffron, and pepper. Bring to a boil, reduce to a simmer, cover and cook, stirring once or twice, for 20 to 25 minutes, until pumpkin is tender. Mash a few pieces of pumpkin with the back of a fork to thicken stew. Serve hot with rice or couscous, if using.

MUSHROOMS AND KALE OVER PUMPKIN POLENTA

I hate to play favorites with my food, but this one really does it for me. Mushrooms seared in butter taste highbrow and professional cheffy, but can easily be created in your own kitchen with a nonstick pan, patience, and a few pats of butter. A golden, pumpkin-packed polenta (or grits) mattress both looks and tastes sufficiently regal to hold such lavishly lacquered vegetables. While this complete-meal is elegant enough to serve as a dinner party main course, it remains fast enough to bring to Tuesday's table after a long day at work.

Serves 4

For the Pumpkin Polenta

2 cups pumpkin purée

1 cup quick-cooking polenta or white hominy grits (smooth and creamy old-fashioned, not instant)

4 cups water or low-sodium vegetable stock

1 tablespoon fresh thyme, chopped, plus more to garnish

1 teaspoon salt

ground black pepper, to taste

2 tablespoons unsalted butter

For the Mushrooms and Kale

2 tablespoons unsalted butter

4 portobello mushrooms, sliced into ¼-inch pieces

4 cups kale, de-stemmed, shredded

1½ tablespoons balsamic vinegar

½ teaspoon salt

For the polenta, in a large pot, whisk all polenta ingredients except butter. Whisking constantly, bring to a boil, reduce to low, cover, and cook for 15 to 20 minutes, whisking every few minutes. Whisk in butter.

For the mushrooms and kale, in a large, nonstick skillet, large skillet, or large cast-iron pan, heat butter over medium/medium-high. Add mushrooms in a single layer and fry on first side for 3 to 5 minutes, until a golden crust develops on bottom side. Flip mushrooms and cook for another 2 to 3 minutes, until soft. Stir in kale, vinegar, and salt; cook until kale is dark green and wilted.

Scoop polenta into bowls and top with mushrooms and kale. Serve immediately.

FIRECRACKER STIR-FRIED PUMPKIN, BOK CHOY, AND CASHEWS

This stir-fry is what I make when I can't face another bowl of cranberry sauce, or sprig of thyme. Tasting and looking like Chinese food take-out—but far healthier and quicker to enjoy—it's a mainstay in my kitchen during the fall and winter months. With just the right amount of sticky-syrupiness and heat, as well as being packed with greens, fat cubes of pumpkin, and swollen-with-flavor cashews, all this peppy dish needs is a mound of rice or noodles to make it a meal.

.... *Serves 2–3* ....

For the Sauce

¼ cup water

2 tablespoons tamari

2 tablespoons rice vinegar

1 teaspoon honey

2 cloves garlic, minced

1 red chili, cut into thin rounds (add less if you prefer a mild sauce)

2 teaspoons arrowroot flour (arrowroot starch)

1 teaspoon ground dried ginger

1 teaspoon five-spice powder

For the Stir-Fry

1 tablespoon coconut oil

½ (2–3 pounds) creamy-fleshed pumpkin such as red kuri or butternut, peeled, seeded, and cut into 1-inch pieces

1 onion, sliced

heaping ½ cup whole raw cashews

1 pound bok choy, quartered

In a small bowl, whisk all sauce ingredients together. Set aside.

In a large wok or large high-sided skillet, heat oil over medium. Add pumpkin and onions; stir, cover, and continue to cook for 10 to 15 minutes, stirring a few times, until pumpkin and onions are tender and beginning to caramelize. Stir in cashews. Add bok choy on top of pumpkin mixture, cover, and cook until bok choy wilts (about 5 minutes). Stir in prepared sauce and cook until all vegetables are tender and sauce is glossy and thick. Serve hot with rice, quinoa, or cellophane noodles.

SOCCA PIZZA WITH ROASTED SQUASH, BRUSSELS SPROUTS, AND LEMON

A giant chickpea flour pancake creates a buttery, gluten-free, high protein crust for an autumnal pizza ready in less than 45 minutes. I often add goat cheese on top and briefly broil to warm, but you could try fresh mozzarella, feta (don't heat), ricotta (don't heat), or keep it off altogether. It's a knife and fork affair, which may disqualify it as pizza; however, classifying this as pizza makes me happy, so it's staying.

Serves 4

For the Vegetables
1 tablespoon extra-virgin olive oil

½ (2–3 pound) creamy-fleshed pumpkin such as kabocha or butternut, seeded, peeled, and cut into ¼-inch cubes

6 ounces Brussels sprouts, quartered

1 onion, thinly sliced

1 teaspoon dried sage (whole, not ground)

½ teaspoon salt

ground black pepper, to taste

For the Socca
1 teaspoon extra-virgin olive oil

2 cups chickpea flour

2 cups water

½ teaspoon salt

1 tablespoon prepared pesto, any variety

zest of 1 lemon

Arrange oven racks to accommodate two dishes. Preheat oven to 400°F.

On a large-rimmed baking sheet, toss to combine all vegetable ingredients. Roast for 30 to 35 minutes, until vegetables are tender and beginning to caramelize. Meanwhile, prepare the socca. Socca goes in the oven halfway through vegetable roasting time.)

Line a large high-sided ceramic skillet or large cast-iron pan with a circle of parchment paper to fit the bottom. Grease parchment circle and sides with oil. In a large bowl, whisk flour, water, and salt until mostly smooth. Pour batter into prepared skillet or pan and bake for 15 minutes (halfway through vegetable roasting time), or until set and beginning to dry out.

To serve, spread socca with pesto, top with vegetables, and garnish with lemon zest. Slice and serve warm or at room temperature.

LASAGNA WITH PUMPKIN ORANGE BÉCHAMEL AND RICOTTA PARMESAN BÉCHAMEL

Unapologetically cheesy, hit with smooth pumpkin and floral orange, this lasagna is the kind of meal to tuck into on the coldest, dreariest nights. Rarely do I create a recipe with so few vegetables, but the good whack of pumpkin in one of the béchamel sauces is all this really needs—maybe a chopped parsley garnish if I'm feeling fussy. To create some balance, a sharp, lemony side salad is a welcome addition to your plate.

Serves 6

For the Ricotta Parmesan Béchamel (base)
2 tablespoons unsalted butter
3 tablespoons unbleached all-purpose flour
3 cups whole milk
1 cup whole milk ricotta
1 cup parmesan, finely grated
½ teaspoon dried oregano
⅛ teaspoon ground nutmeg
salt and ground black pepper, to taste

For the Pumpkin Orange Béchamel
1 cup Ricotta Parmesan Béchamel (from above)
1⅔ cups pumpkin purée
1 teaspoon orange zest

For Assembly
1 (14-ounce) package whole grain lasagna noodles, cooked according to package directions; drained, rinsed with cold water, and drained again

To make the base béchamel, in a large pot, melt butter over medium heat. Whisk in flour and cook until fragrant. Whisking constantly, slowly add milk until fully incorporated. Continue to cook, whisking constantly, until mixture is thick and bubbly. Remove from heat and whisk in ricotta, parmesan, oregano, nutmeg, salt, and pepper.

To make the pumpkin béchamel, scoop 1 cup base béchamel into a medium bowl and whisk in pumpkin purée and orange zest.

Preheat oven to 375°F.

To assemble, spread a layer of pumpkin béchamel on the bottom of a medium to large glass or ceramic casserole dish. Add a layer of noodles and repeat alternating layers of base béchamel, noodles, and pumpkin béchamel, finishing with remaining base and pumpkin béchamel to cover the top noodles. Cover with parchment-lined foil and bake for 45 minutes; uncover and bake for an addition 15 to 25 minutes, until bubbling. Leave oven rack and lasagna in center position; turn on broiler and broil until golden brown on top (2 to 5 minutes). Rest for 5 minutes before slicing and serving.

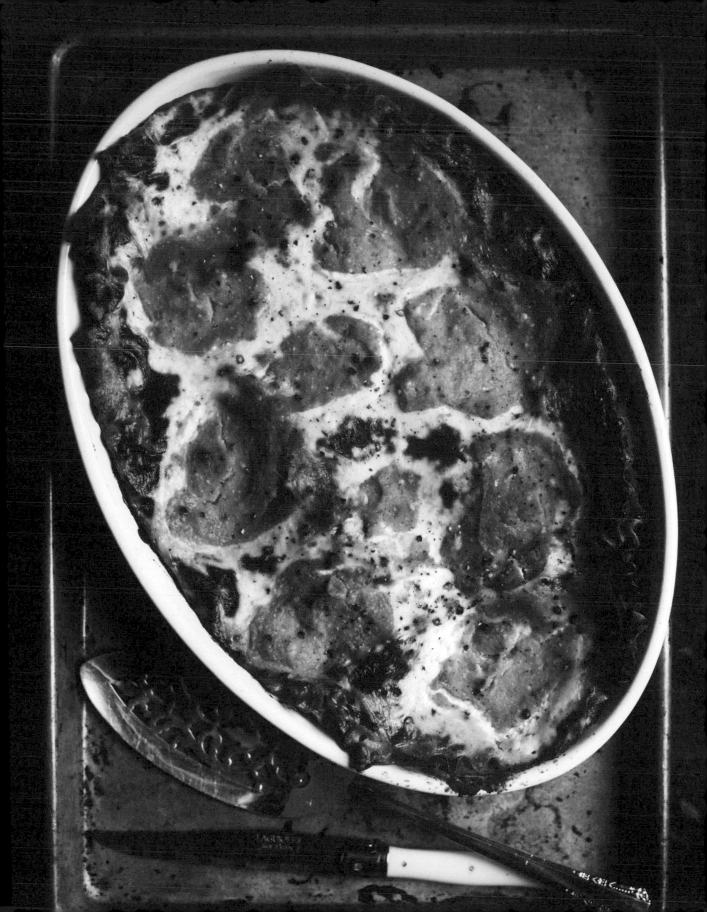

VEGAN PUMPKIN, ONION, AND SPINACH LASAGNA WITH WHITE BEAN RICOTTA

I recall my mom using the term *labor of love* when referring to lasagna, making me think it had to be complicated to be good—but it really doesn't. This pumpkin lasagna is fast (it's a bit of a cheater's recipe, really), fresh, and tastes quintessentially autumnal in each savory layer. At our house, lasagna was always served with Caesar salad, and likely, this version would get the same treatment; I'd try the pumpkin-spiked Caesar a few chapters back (see page **123**) if you were to go this route.

Serves 4–5

For the Pumpkin Layer
1 tablespoon extra-virgin olive oil
2 onions, thinly sliced
2 cloves garlic, minced
2½ cups pumpkin purée
1 tablespoon white wine vinegar
½ teaspoon salt
1 teaspoon dried thyme

For the White Bean Ricotta
1 (19-ounce) can white beans, drained and rinsed
1 teaspoon fresh rosemary, chopped
1 tablespoon lemon juice, plus more to serve
ground black pepper, to taste

For Assembly
Approximately 12 (about ½ of a 14-ounce package) oven-ready whole grain lasagna noodles
2 cups packed, pre-washed baby spinach
1 cup fresh basil leaves

Preheat oven to 350°F.

For the pumpkin layer, in a large high-sided skillet, heat oil over medium. Add onion and garlic, reduce heat to medium-low; sauté for 10 minutes, until onions are soft and beginning to brown. Stir in pumpkin, vinegar, salt, and thyme. Set aside.

For the white bean ricotta, in a food processor, blend all ricotta ingredients until pale and creamy (about 1 to 2 minutes). Set aside.

To assemble, spread a thin layer of pumpkin mixture on the bottom of an 8 x 8–inch baking dish or metal pan. Add a layer of 3 noodles (you'll have to break to fit). Top with ⅓ of the pumpkin mixture; spread to cover. Add a layer of 3 noodles (break to fit). Dollop ½ of ricotta; spread to cover. Add a layer of 3 noodles (break to fit). Sprinkle over spinach and gently press. Top with ⅓ of the pumpkin mixture; spread to cover. Add a layer of 3 noodles (break to fit). Dollop remaining ½ of ricotta; spread to cover. Top with remaining ⅓ of the pumpkin mixture; spread to cover. Top pumpkin with basil leaves. Cover with parchment then seal with foil.

Bake lasagna for 1 hour. Remove parchment and foil. Bake for an additional 5 to 10 minutes. Let rest for 5 to 10 minutes before slicing with a serrated knife. Serve hot with lemon for spritzing (a drizzle of aged balsamic is equally nice).

CURRIED PUMPKIN TOFU CALZONES

A take on the Italian calzone, this Indian-inspired meal gets the pizza-pocket treatment, resulting in pillows of piping-hot comfort food. If you don't like the idea of tofu, replace it with chickpeas or cubes of cooked chicken breast—any neutral, tender protein will work in harmony with the powerful tastes here. A handful of frozen, defrosted peas feels quite at home in these as well.

Makes 4 large calzones

½ recipe Spelt Pizza Dough (see page **159**), rolled according to dough directions into 4 large circles

2 tablespoons coconut oil, plus more for brushing

3 cloves garlic, minced

2 cups pumpkin purée or roughly mashed pumpkin, room temperature

1 (12-ounce) package extra-firm tofu, drained, pressed, and cut into small cubes

1 cup cilantro, chopped

½ red chili, minced

1 tablespoon lemon juice

1 tablespoon curry powder (mild or hot)

2 teaspoons garam masala

1 teaspoon salt, plus more to taste

Preheat oven to 425°F. Arrange oven racks to accommodate 2 baking sheets. Dust 2 large baking sheets with a bit of spelt flour. Place 2 pieces of rolled dough on each baking sheet.

In a small saucepan, heat coconut oil over medium. Add garlic and cook for 30 seconds until fragrant. Add to a large mixing bowl with remaining ingredients. Mix well. Taste filling and season with additional salt if necessary.

Leaving a ½ to 1-inch border, top half of each piece of dough with filling, firmly shaping into a half-moon. Fold over other half and close calzones by twisting dough so it seals together (it doesn't have to be perfect—mine certainly aren't—just make sure it's closed). Brush with a little melted coconut oil or olive oil. Bake for 20 to 25 minutes until puffed and crust is crispy when knocked on. Slice in half with a serrated knife and serve hot, at room temperature, or chilled.

DESSERTS

While I hope I've convinced you that pumpkin can be enjoyed in infinite savory ways, the ways many us are most familiar with, and our first introductions to this squash, are generally via dessert. Pumpkin's inherent sweetness plays beautifully with the season's warming spices like cinnamon and nutmeg (and pumpkin spice) and is brought out further by complex sugars like maple syrup and honey. Of course, pumpkin pie is included—not that you needed another pumpkin pie recipe, but because it would seem sacrilegious to do without one in this cookbook—and is up there with my top picks for this chapter's tastiest treats (it's a classic for a reason!). And if I were to continue to play favorites, the pumpkin cheesecake is my personal top pick because firstly, I am human, and secondly, it's cheesecake. Beyond pie and cheesecake, you're spoiled for choice; baked donuts, cookies, creamy treats, chocolaty bites, and more, for any hankering. Here's to pumpkin dessert stalwarts and new-classics; may they add a touch of special occasion to any special occasion, or the everyday.

RECIPES

CLASSIC PUMPKIN PIE

203

MINI CLASSIC PUMPKIN PIES

204

PUMPKIN SEED OIL SHORTBREAD
JAM SQUARES

207

COOKIES OF PLENTY WITH
CHOCOLATE, PUMPKIN,
CRANBERRIES, AND PUMPKIN
SEEDS

208

CHOCOLATE PUMPKIN SEED
BUTTER CUPS

211

GINGERBREAD PUMPKIN
CHEESECAKE WITH PECAN OAT
CRUST

213

BROWN BUTTER AND SAFFRON
WHOLE WHEAT PUMPKIN
CUSTARD CAKE

215

STICKY TOFFEE PUMPKIN SPICE
PECAN TRUFFLES

217

PUMPKIN SPICE RUGELACH WITH
CHESTNUT JAM

218

HOMEMADE PUMPKIN BUTTER
POPTARTS

221

FUDGY PUMPKIN COFFEE
BROWNIES

222

PUMPKIN CARDAMOM DONUTS
WITH CHAI GLAZE

225

SPELT PUMPKIN SPICE
GINGERBREAD FOREST ANIMAL
COOKIES

227

CRANBERRY-PUMPKIN CLAFOUTIS
WITH OAT FLOUR

230

SALTED HONEY PUMPKIN CRÈME
BRÛLÉE

233

VEGAN COCONUT, VANILLA BEAN,
AND PUMPKIN PANNA COTTA

234

DULCE DE LECHE PUMPKIN
MOUSSE

237

CLASSIC PUMPKIN PIE

A pumpkin cookbook without a classic pumpkin pie recipe would be unwise, but I knew it had to be the best pumpkin pie or my name would be mud. My version, spiced and sweetened to perfection (if I do say so myself) is what I imagined classic pumpkin pie would be.

.... *Makes 1 pie, serves 8* ....

For the Dough
1 Spelt Pie Crust (½ recipe) (see page **244**)
light or dark spelt flour, for rolling

For the Filling
1¾ cups pumpkin purée

1½ cups evaporated milk
3 large eggs
¾ cup packed demerara sugar (dark brown sugar)
2 teaspoons pumpkin spice (see page **247**)
½ teaspoon salt
whipped cream, for serving

Preheat oven to 375°F.

Roll dough on a floured surface with a floured rolling pin into a large circle about 1 inch larger than your pie plate, until ¼ to ½ inch in thickness. Fold dough in half and place in pie plate, pressing gently to fit in. Trim loose edges and tuck remaining under the edge, crimping with your fingers or fork. Freeze until solid (about 30 minutes). Meanwhile, prepare the filling.

In a large bowl, whisk all filling ingredients together until fully combined. Remove crust from freezer and pour filling until only 1 inch of crust (the crimped edges) is visible. You can use any leftover filling for Mini Classic Pumpkin Pies (see page **204**) or bake in ramekins for a crust-free, gluten-free variation).

Carefully transfer pie to oven and bake for 55 to 65 minutes until crust is crisp and filling is just-set, slightly puffed, and a knife inserted in the center comes out mostly clean (tap the side of the pie—it should only jiggle a little). Cool completely. Chill covered in refrigerator for up to 3 days (crust will be best on the first or second day). Slice and serve chilled or at room temperature with whipped cream.

NOTES

To bake pie crust scraps, preheat oven to 375°F. Place scraps on a large-rimmed baking sheet and bake for 15 to 20 minutes, or until golden and puffed. Makes a nice little snack dipped into whipped cream (for the baker, of course). You can also cut them into shapes and use to garnish your pie.

MINI CLASSIC PUMPKIN PIES

This is pretty much Pumpkin Pie Jr. These festive morsels are ideal for entertaining. Set up an interactive toppings bar for you and your guests to garnish with abandon.

.... *Makes 12 mini pies* ....

1 Spelt Pie Crust (½ recipe) (see page **244**)
light or dark spelt flour, for rolling
1 recipe Classic Pumpkin Pie filling (see page **203**)

Topping Ideas
whipped cream
plain Greek yogurt spiked with orange liquor and orange zest

melted dark chocolate or chocolate chips
baked Spelt Pie Crust scraps (see *Notes*)
pecans or walnuts
chopped roasted chestnuts
roasted pumpkin seeds
maple syrup
demerara sugar (dark brown sugar)

Preheat oven to 375°F.

Roll dough on a floured surface with a floured rolling pin into a large circle ¼ to ½ inch in thickness. Using a 4-inch cookie cutter or large rim of a glass, cut rounds and transfer to a standard muffin tin, gently pressing to fit in. Repeat rolling and cutting with remaining scraps. Roll any odd scraps and cut into small rounds to bake later for use as a topping. Freeze dough in muffin pan until solid (about 30 minutes).

Fill frozen shells with 2½ to 3 tablespoons of filling (there will likely be leftover, which you can bake in ramekins or make more mini pies with). Bake for 20 to 30 minutes, until crust is crisp and filling is just-set, slightly puffed, and a knife inserted in the center comes out mostly clean (tap the side of the muffin tins—the centers should only jiggle a little). Cool completely in muffin tin. Using a paring knife, run around the edges of the crust and pop out. Transfer pies to a serving platter.

Set up a topping bar where guests can adorn their mini pies as they like. Serve at room temperature or chilled.

> **NOTES**
>
> To bake pie crust scraps, preheat oven to 375°F. Place scraps on a large-rimmed baking sheet and bake for 15 to 20 minutes, or until golden and puffed. Makes a nice little snack dipped into whipped cream (for the baker only, of course), or for garnishing your pie.

PUMPKIN SEED OIL SHORTBREAD JAM SQUARES

Shortbreads are a holiday cookie requisite, as lovely to gift as they are to gorge on. I've worked pumpkin seed oil into the traditional melt-in-your-mouth, buttery shortbread dough, lending a tawny hue and mellow nutty taste. These are a one-bowl affair that come together in a snap, though the cooling time is excruciating as they tease you on the counter with their deliriously buttery aroma. However, as a holiday baking rule, corners that have "fallen off" while cooling are the cook's treat.

Makes 12 squares

¼ cup unsalted butter, room temperature

½ cup light brown sugar, lightly packed

¼ cup pumpkin seed oil

1 tablespoon vanilla extract

1⅓ cups unbleached all-purpose flour or light spelt flour

¼ cup arrowroot flour (arrowroot starch)

½ teaspoon salt

½ cup high-quality cherry jam or jam flavor of choice

Preheat oven to 350°F. Line an 8 x 8–inch square baking pan with parchment paper, leaving some overhang.

In a large bowl with a spatula or wooden spoon, cream butter and sugar until pale. Using a whisk, whisk in pumpkin seed oil and vanilla until fully combined. Switch back to a spatula or wooden spoon and stir in flour, arrowroot, and salt until fully combined. Transfer dough to prepared pan and firmly press into bottom using your fingers or the bottom of a measuring cup. Evenly spread top of dough with jam. Bake for 30 minutes. Cool for 20 minutes in pan. Run a sharp knife around the edges and remove shortbread; transfer to a wire rack to cool completely. Slice into 12 squares. Store at room temperature or freeze airtight for up to 1 month.

COOKIES OF PLENTY WITH CHOCOLATE, PUMPKIN, CRANBERRIES, AND PUMPKIN SEEDS

These cookies happen to be gluten-free. They don't really don't go around parading that, though, and certainly don't taste "free" of anything found in traditional baking. They're perfect cookies jam-packed with the season's best.

.... *Makes 25–30 cookies* ....

¾ cup unsalted butter

⅔ cup packed demerara sugar (dark brown sugar)

2 teaspoons vanilla extract

2 extra-large eggs

½ cup pumpkin purée

2 cups large-flake rolled oats (not instant)

1 cup buckwheat flour

¾ cup brown rice flour

1 cup sweetened dried cranberries

½ cup semisweet or dark chocolate chips

½ cup raw, unsalted green pumpkin seeds

1 tablespoon pumpkin spice (see page **247**)

½ teaspoon baking powder

½ teaspoon baking soda

½ teaspoon xanthan gum

½ teaspoon salt

Arrange oven racks to accommodate 2 baking sheets. Preheat oven to 375°F.

In a stand mixer fitted with a paddle attachment, or by hand in a large bowl with a spatula, cream butter and sugar together until smooth. Add eggs and vanilla and mix until fluffy. Mix in pumpkin.

In a large bowl, mix together remaining dry ingredients. Stir dry ingredients into butter mixture and mix until fully incorporated. Portion cookie dough into 2½ to 3 tablespoon-sized balls, 2 inches apart, onto a large-rimmed baking sheet (you'll have to bake in batches). Bake cookies for 7 minutes, rotate pans (bottom pan now on top, top pan now on bottom), and bake for 7 to 8 minutes longer. Cool on a wire rack and store airtight at room temperature. Baked cookies and unbaked dough can both be frozen for up to 3 months.

CHOCOLATE PUMPKIN SEED BUTTER CUPS

A gooier, healthier, peanut-free take on the peanut butter cups kids fill old pillowcases with on Halloween, looking a bit spookier with their murky green interior to boot. Like their appearance, their taste does not mess around, being intensely (and unapologetically) chocolaty and ultra rich, so much so that I use a chef's knife to slice them in half when chilled. I love the cups straight out of the freezer with a jet-black espresso or coffee for an afternoon jolt; for kids, a glass of milk is probably a better option.

If you don't have time to make pumpkin seed butter, purchase natural, no sugar or salt added pumpkin seed butter, peanut butter, or almond butter to use instead.

Makes 6 large or 12 small cups

8 ounces dark or semisweet chocolate, roughly chopped
½ cup Pumpkin Seed Butter (see page **251**)
¼ cup maple syrup
½ teaspoon vanilla extract

½ teaspoon pumpkin spice (see page **247**)
¼ teaspoon salt
crunchy toppings of choice (roasted pumpkin seeds, sprinkles, coconut, etc.)

Line a standard muffin tin with 6 to 12 large muffin papers (depending if you want them mammoth-sized or thinner), or a mini muffin tin with mini muffin papers.

In a double boiler, melt chocolate over medium-low heat. Divide half of the chocolate amongst muffin papers, slightly pulling chocolate up the sides. Freeze for 10 minutes.

In a medium bowl, mix pumpkin seed butter, maple syrup, vanilla, pumpkin spice, and salt. Divide between cold chocolate bottoms, smoothing out top of mixture with your finger. Cover pumpkin seed butter mixture with remaining chocolate, smoothing top gently (as to not mix filling and chocolate). Sprinkle with crunchy toppings of choice and freeze for at least 1 hour. Store in refrigerator for up to 2 weeks or freezer for up to 2 months.

GINGERBREAD PUMPKIN CHEESECAKE WITH PECAN OAT CRUST

Loving cheesecake is the human condition. It's one of the foods I lust after, but rarely prepare, making its enjoyment all the more special. The thin, cookie-like crust is a play on buttered pecans, perfumed with the nut, oats that get toasty, and a bit of butter. (It's also gluten-free!) The delicately gingered filling is velvety and dense, more New York–style than ethereal—it doesn't mess around, nor should it. Pumpkin cheesecake gives the pie a run for its money (but I'll take both, happily, and on one plate).

Serves 10–12

For the Pecan Oat Crust

1 cup quick-cooking rolled oats, divided

½ cup pecans, chopped

¼ cup unsalted butter, melted

1 tablespoon molasses

½ teaspoon salt

For the Gingerbread Pumpkin Cheesecake Filling

3 (8-ounce/250-gram) bricks full-fat cream cheese, room temperature (preferably leave out overnight)

¾ cups light brown sugar, packed

1 cup pumpkin purée, room temperature

1 tablespoon molasses

1 tablespoon vanilla extract

1 tablespoon pumpkin spice (see page **247**), plus more for serving

1 teaspoon ground dried ginger

¼ teaspoon salt

4 large eggs, room temperature

For the crust, preheat oven to 350°F. In a food processor or blender, blend ½ cup oats with pecans until finely ground. Add to a large bowl with remaining ½ cup oats (unblended), butter, molasses, and salt. Mix until combined. Press into the bottom of a 9-inch nonstick springform pan (the crust is to be thin). Bake for 15 minutes. Place on a large-rimmed baking sheet and set aside to cool completely while preparing filling.

For the filling, turn oven down to 300°F. In the bowl of a stand mixer fitted with a paddle attachment or in a large bowl with a handheld mixer, beat cream cheese until smooth; scrape down sides and paddle, or scrape down beaters and beat again. Beat in brown sugar; scrape down sides and paddle, or scrape down beaters and beat again. Beat in pumpkin, molasses, vanilla, pumpkin spice, ginger, and salt; scrape down sides and paddle, or scrape down beaters and beat again. Add eggs one at a time, beating on low until incorporated. Pour mixture into prepared crust and bake for 1 hour and 15 minutes. Turn oven off and let sit for 30 minutes. Remove from oven and cool completely to room temperature; refrigerate for at least 8 hours (or preferably overnight) until cold.

To serve, run a sharp knife around rim of cheesecake; unhinge pan, sprinkle very lightly with additional pumpkin spice, if desired, and slice. Serve chilled.

BROWN BUTTER AND SAFFRON WHOLE WHEAT PUMPKIN CUSTARD CAKE

Custard cake is like pulling a rabbit out of a top hat—magic! Once baked, the cake separates into a light, pumpkin cake bottom and pumpkin custard top. Browning the butter beforehand adds a metaphorical layer of deep, nutty flavor. Finally, deeply orange saffron threads lend an earthy, Moroccan flare. A dollop of yogurt and sprinkle of slivered almonds or pistachios on top is how I like to serve this—a cup of mint tea doesn't hurt, either.

.... *Serves 9* ....

½ cup unsalted butter

1 cup whole milk or unsweetened plain soy milk

1 cup pumpkin purée

1 tablespoon vanilla extract

4 eggs, separated

⅔ cup light brown sugar, lightly packed

½ teaspoon baking soda

¼ teaspoon saffron

¼ teaspoon salt

1 cup whole wheat pastry flour

plain yogurt, for serving (optional)

slivered almonds or chopped pistachios, for serving (optional)

Preheat oven to 325°F. Line an 8 x 8– or 9 x 9–inch square pan with parchment paper, leaving some overhang.

In a small skillet, melt butter over medium heat. Continue to cook over medium heat until light brown and nutty (2 to 3 minutes). Immediately transfer to a bowl (including brown bits). Set aside to cool slightly. Add brown butter to a large bowl or measuring cup with a pouring spout and whisk in milk, pumpkin, and vanilla.

In a stand mixer fitted with a whisk attachment or in a large bowl with a hand mixer, whip egg whites until firm peaks form. Transfer to a clean bowl. Add egg yolks, sugar, baking soda, saffron, and salt to the stand mixer or the large bowl the egg whites were in (no need to clean). Beat until pale yellow and thick. To egg yolks, slowly beat in brown butter and pumpkin mixture. Add flour and beat on low until combined; scrape down sides, and briefly beat again until fully incorporated. Remove bowl from stand mixer, if using.

With a large rubber spatula by hand, fold in half of reserved egg whites. Fold in remaining half until fully incorporated. Pour into prepared pan and smooth out top. Bake for 40 to 45 minutes, until cake is puffed and still slightly wobbly in the center. Cool completely in pan on a wire rack. Refrigerate for at least 4 hours before loosening edges and removing cake from pan using parchment overhang. Slice into squares or rectangles and serve chilled with a dollop of yogurt and sprinkle of nuts, if using.

STICKY TOFFEE PUMPKIN SPICE PECAN TRUFFLES

Raw, vegan energy bites masquerading as candy? I'm in. These sticky, cocoa-smacked orbs are a healthy snack to keep in your repertoire, all year long.

.... *Makes 12–14* ....

1 cup raw pecan halves
2 tablespoons raw cacao powder or unsweetened cocoa powder
2 teaspoons pumpkin spice (see page **247**)
pinch, salt
10 medjool dates, pitted (preferably very fresh, juicy ones)
½ teaspoon vanilla extract

Pulse pecans, cacao or cocoa, pumpkin spice, and salt until finely chopped. Add dates and vanilla; pulse until fully incorporated (you may need to stop and scrape down sides). Line a plate with waxed or parchment paper and roll into 12 to 14 truffles. Store airtight in the refrigerator for up to 2 weeks.

PUMPKIN SPICE RUGELACH WITH CHESTNUT JAM

Rugelach, a traditional Jewish treat, is a holiday cookie tin staple. Tender, crisp-chewy cream cheese dough is smacked with warming pumpkin spice and coiled around chestnut jam. If you can't find chestnut jam, any thick jam or spread will do the trick. If you're feeling dangerous, a dusting of chopped dark chocolate feels right at home between the sheets.

Makes 36

½ cup unsalted butter, room temperature

7 ounces (nearly 1 (8-ounce) brick) full-fat cream cheese, room temperature

½ cup light brown sugar, lightly packed

2 teaspoons vanilla extract

1 tablespoon pumpkin spice (see page **247**)

½ teaspoon salt

1⅔ cups unbleached all-purpose flour, plus more, for rolling

⅔ cup high-quality chestnut jam such as Bonne Maman or jam of choice (raspberry and blueberry are both lovely)

In a stand mixer fitted with a paddle attachment or in a large bowl by hand, beat butter to soften. Add cream cheese and beat again until smooth. Add sugar and cream until light brown (about 1 minute). Scrape down sides, add vanilla, pumpkin spice, and salt, and beat again until light and fluffy. Scrape down sides, and beat again until fully combined. With the mixer running on low or stirring in gradually by hand, add flour, mixing until a ragged dough is formed. Transfer dough to 2 large pieces of plastic wrap, shape into 1-inch-high discs, and refrigerate until firm (about 2 hours).

Preheat oven to 350°F. Line 2 large-rimmed baking sheets with parchment paper.

Roll 1 dough disc (it may need to sit at room temperature for a few minutes to soften) between 2 sheets of wax or parchment paper into a rough circle ¼ inch thick. Spread 1/3 cup chestnut spread of jam over entire surface. Using a sharp knife, cut into quarters; cut each of the quarters into quarters for 16 triangles. Roll into a coil from the edge of each triangle to the point; place on prepared baking sheet; repeat with remaining triangles. Refrigerate for 10 minutes, or until firm, and repeat with other disc of dough and remaining 1/3 cup chestnut spread or jam, placing those rugelach on the other prepared baking sheet.

Bake first tray of rugelach for 20 to 25 minutes, until golden brown on the bottom and dry to the touch. Cool completely on baking sheet. Repeat with second tray. Store airtight at room temperature or freeze for up to 2 months.

HOMEMADE PUMPKIN BUTTER POPTARTS

I was never allowed actual pop-tarts as a child, something I should probably be thankful for, as they're not good for you, nor do they taste good, which I learned in adulthood. Something else I discovered in adulthood (without getting too X-rated) is the fact that pop-tarts are just turnovers or hand-pies, which I had plenty of in my youth (confounding, no?). And a hand-pie is even easier to make than an actual pie, making their inclusion necessary in both this chapter and my life.

Makes 8

For the Pumpkin Butter Poptarts
1 Spelt Pie Crust (½ recipe) (see page **244**)
light or dark spelt flour, for rolling
1 cup Pumpkin Butter (see page **248**)

For the Pumpkin Spice Drizzle
⅓ cup icing sugar, sifted
¼ teaspoon pumpkin spice (see page **247**)
1 tablespoon evaporated milk or whole milk

Preheat oven to 400°F. Line a large-rimmed baking sheet with parchment paper.

Roll dough on a floured surface with a floured rolling pin into large rectangle until ¼ to ½ inch in thickness. Trim rough edges with a crimping wheel or paring knife. Cut into 3 x 3–inch squares.

Add 2 teaspoons pumpkin butter to the center of half of the squares. Fill squares with a plain square of dough and crimp to seal with a fork around the edges (if a little filling gets out, don't panic, it'll be just fine). Place filled squares 1 inch apart on prepared baking sheet and freeze until solid (about 30 minutes). Re-roll scraps; repeat cutting and filling with remaining dough (they can be smaller or larger, and any odd shape works—even a single piece to make a "turnover").

Bake for 20 to 25 minutes, until puffed and beginning to slightly brown. Cool on baking sheet for 5 minutes before transferring to a wire rack to cool completely.

For the glaze, whisk all glaze ingredients in a small bowl until smooth. Drizzle glaze over cooled pop-tarts and allow to set for at least 2 hours. Store in a covered glass casserole dish at room temperature.

FUDGY PUMPKIN COFFEE BROWNIES

The good news? Pumpkin purée's addition reduces the total amount of butter and sugar you have to use to get that classic, fudgy crumb many of us love in brownies. And, if you can say the title five times fast, you get the whole pan. The bad news? These are brownies; there is no bad news.

.... *Makes 12* ....

¼ cup plus 1 tablespoon unsalted butter

6 ounces (about 1 cup) dark chocolate or chocolate chips, chopped

½ cup plus 2 tablespoons evaporated cane sugar

¾ cup pumpkin purée

2 eggs

¼ teaspoon almond extract or vanilla extract

2 tablespoons finely ground coffee

2 teaspoons pumpkin spice (see page **247**)

¼ teaspoon salt

¾ cup einkorn flour or light spelt flour

Preheat oven to 350°F. Line an 8 x 8–inch square baking pan with parchment paper, leaving some overhang.

In a medium saucepan, melt butter. Remove from heat, add chocolate, and allow residual heat to melt chocolate (if it needs it, a very low heat is okay, just be sure to keep stirring). Mix in sugar, followed by pumpkin purée, followed by eggs, extract, coffee, pumpkin spice, and salt. Stir in flour until just incorporated and pour into prepared pan, smoothing out top with an offset spatula.

Bake for 20 to 25 minutes, until set but still fudgy in the center. Cool for 5 minutes in pan. Remove from pan using parchment overhang and transfer to a wire rack to cool completely. Slice into 12 squares. Store airtight in refrigerator for up to 2 weeks or freezer for up to 2 months.

PUMPKIN CARDAMOM DONUTS WITH CHAI GLAZE

Pumpkin purée adds moisture and a glorious sunflower-yellow, sunglasses-required tint to these baked (not fried) vegan bites. Perked up with a spicy chai blend, they feel very grown up, miles away from Homer Simpson's iconic, pink-frosted with sprinkles loop.

Nonstick donut pans are a bit of a novelty kitchen item, but a fairly inexpensive one at that; I bought mine online for about fifteen dollars.

.... *Makes 14–16 mini donuts* ....

Pumpkin Cardamom Donuts

1 cup light spelt flour

½ cup evaporated cane sugar

1 teaspoon baking powder

1 teaspoon ground cardamom

½ teaspoon salt

1 cup pumpkin purée

¼ cup coconut oil, melted, plus more to grease pans

3 tablespoons unsweetened plain soy milk

½ teaspoon almond extract

Chai Glaze

1 cup icing sugar, sifted

½ teaspoon ground dried ginger

¼ teaspoon ground cardamom

⅛ teaspoon ground cloves

⅛ teaspoon ground cinnamon

a few grinds of black pepper

2 tablespoons unsweetened plain soy milk

½ teaspoon vanilla extract

Preheat oven to 375°F. Grease a 12-count mini nonstick donut pan (you will have to bake in 2 batches).

For the donuts, in a large bowl, combine flour, sugar, baking powder, cardamom, and salt. In a medium bowl, combine pumpkin, oil, milk, and almond extract; stir into flour mixture and mix until combined. Transfer mixture to a large zip-top bag (or use a large pastry bag), seal, and cut a 1-inch slice in the corner to squeeze donut batter into pan. Fill each donut round to the top. Bake for 10–12 minutes, until a toothpick inserted in the center comes out clean. Immediately flip out onto a wire cooling rack. Repeat with remaining batter. Cool completely.

For the glaze, in a medium bowl, whisk all ingredients together until smooth. Dip the tops of the cooled donuts in glaze, return to wire rack, and allow to set at room temperature for at least 2 hours. Store airtight at room temperature.

SPELT PUMPKIN SPICE GINGERBREAD FOREST ANIMAL COOKIES

Whimsical forest creatures (or traditional gingerbread people) come to life with this peppery spice cookie, which are as delicious plain as they are gussied up with a few fabulous, festive trimmings.

..... *Makes 2 discs of cookie dough (amount of cookies dependent on shape and size)* ....

For the Cookies

2 cups light spelt flour

1 cup whole wheat pastry flour, plus more for rolling

1 tablespoon ground dried ginger

2 teaspoons pumpkin spice (see page **247**)

¼ teaspoon baking soda

¼ teaspoon salt

½ cup unsalted butter, room temperature

⅓ cup light brown sugar, packed

1 large egg

⅓ cup molasses

For the Icing and Decorations

3 tablespoons plus 1 teaspoon water

2 tablespoons meringue powder

2 cups confectioner's (icing) sugar, sifted

all-natural gel or powdered food coloring (optional)

assorted edible sugar embellishments (optional)

For the cookies, in a medium bowl, combine flours, ginger, pumpkin spice, baking soda, and salt. In a stand mixer fitted with a paddle attachment or in a large bowl by hand, beat butter to soften. Add sugar and cream until light brown (about 1 minute). Scrape down sides and add molasses and egg. Beat until light and fluffy, scrape down sides, and beat again until fully combined. With the mixer running on low or stirring in gradually by hand, add flour mixture, mixing until combined. Transfer dough to 2 large pieces of plastic wrap, shape into 1-inch-high discs, and refrigerate until firm (about 2 hours).

Remove dough from refrigerator to warm up just a bit. Preheat oven to 350ºF. Line 2 large-rimmed baking sheets with parchment paper. (You'll need to bake in batches, so if you just have a single baking sheet, that works, too.) Place a large piece of parchment paper on the counter and lightly sprinkle with a bit of whole wheat pastry flour; add one of the dough discs, sprinkle the disc lightly with more flour, and place another piece of parchment on top. Roll to ¼ inch thickness using a rolling pin. Cut out into forest animal cookie cutter shapes or classic gingerbread people or any shape your heart desires. Place at least ½ inch apart on prepared baking sheet. Chill for 5 minutes in refrigerator. Repeat with dough scraps. Remove first cookie sheet from refrigerator, working one sheet of cookies at a time for 12 to 15 minutes, until slightly puffed and crispy on the bottom. Let sit on cookie sheet for 2 to 3 minutes; transfer to a wire rack to cool completely. Repeat with rolled out cookie scraps and other disc of dough.

For the icing, in a medium bowl, whisk water and meringue powder until glossy, fluffy, and white. Slowly whisk in sifted icing sugar. Keep plain or separate into small ramekins and tint with food coloring, if desired. Frost and decorate cooled cookies however you like. Allow frosting to harden completely on cookies for at least 8 hours, preferably overnight. Store airtight at room temperature for up to 2 weeks.

NOTES

Freeze unbaked dough discs for up to 2 months; freeze baked, unfrosted cookies for up to 1 month.

CRANBERRY-PUMPKIN CLAFOUTIS WITH OAT FLOUR

In university, I remember being given a piece of clafoutis by my landlord before heading out on a (bad) date. My landlord made traditional cherry-almond clafoutis, and I adored it, having never eaten anything quite like it before. It seemed very chic and, therefore, hard to pull off, but I learned clafoutis is merely a one-bowl eggy custard baked pancake (read: easy). It's only a little bit sweet so don't expect a birthday cake–type sugar buzz from this dessert. Here, I've made the clafoutis holiday-appropriate with a pumpkin batter base and puckery cranberry crown.

······································· *Serves 4–6* ·······································

½ cup pumpkin purée
3 large eggs
⅓ cup light brown sugar, packed
1 cup milk of choice
1 tablespoon vanilla extract
¼ teaspoon almond extract
⅓ cup oat flour
⅛ teaspoon salt
1 cup fresh or frozen cranberries
confectioner's (icing) sugar, for dusting (optional)

Preheat oven to 375°F.

In a medium bowl, whisk pumpkin and eggs; whisk in brown sugar, followed by milk and extracts. Whisk in oat flour and salt until combined; keep mixing until there are no large lumps from the oat flour (a few small ones are okay). Pour into an 8- to 10-inch ceramic or glass pie plate or an 8 x 8–inch ceramic or glass baking dish. Top with cranberries. Bake for 35 to 45 minutes, until only still slightly jiggling in the center and light brown on top. Dust with confectioners' sugar, if using. Serve warm, at room temperature, or chilled.

SALTED HONEY PUMPKIN CRÈME BRÛLÉE

Floral honey is a much softer pairing for sea salt than caramel, imbuing its delicate, ornamental qualities to sweet cream and pumpkin. Crème brûlée is not as froufrou as you may think—a few easy-but-required steps are all that's needed, and I've outlined them below. What's more, crème brûlée is a make-ahead dessert, freeing up oven space for any holiday entertaining you may do. I've kept the baked custards (without the crunchy sugar top) tightly covered with plastic wrap in the refrigerator for 3 days, and neither taste nor texture suffered.

Serves 4

2 large eggs
1 teaspoon vanilla extract
½ teaspoon ground dried ginger
¼ teaspoon sea salt, plus more for sugar top
⅛ teaspoon ground nutmeg

1 cup plus 2 tablespoons heavy whipping cream
½ cup pumpkin purée
¼ cup honey
2 tablespoons granulated sugar

Preheat oven to 325°F.

In a large bowl or extra-large liquid measuring cup with a pouring spout, whisk together eggs, vanilla, ginger, salt, and nutmeg. In a medium saucepan, whisk together cream, pumpkin, and honey; heat over medium until it's too hot to leave your finger in comfortably (look for a few bubbles around the outside). Using a fine mesh sieve, strain a couple tablespoons hot cream mixture into egg mixture to temper; whisk together. Strain remaining hot cream mixture into egg mixture; whisk together.

Boil a kettle of water. Place 4 (4-ounce) ovenproof ramekins in a large glass dish or deep baking sheet. Divide cream mixture between ramekins (approximately ½ cup in each ramekin) using a ladle or the measuring cup spout. Carefully pour hot water around ramekins, being sure not to splash water in the cream mixture, until it reaches 1/3 to ½ way up the sides of the ramekins. Open the oven door and gently place glass dish or baking sheet in oven. Bake for 20 to 25 minutes, until cream mixture only slightly jiggles when tapped. Remove ramekins from water and cool to room temperature on a wire rack; transfer to refrigerator to cool completely (about 5 hours or overnight).

To brûlée, sprinkle 1 to 2 teaspoons sugar and a pinch of salt over custards; caramelize sugar using a kitchen blowtorch or place ramekins on a large baking sheet and broil until sugar is caramelized to your liking. Serve.

VEGAN COCONUT, VANILLA BEAN, AND PUMPKIN PANNA COTTA

A traditional Italian dessert is made vegan with non-dairy milk and agar-agar, a tasteless sea vegetable that can replace teaspoon for teaspoon with gelatin (an animal product). If you'd like to make this taste like pumpkin pie, add the pumpkin spice or cinnamon I've suggested; if you prefer a cleaner taste, skip the spices altogether, allowing the pumpkin, vanilla bean, and milk to shine through. A tumble of fresh raspberries or scoop of sticky raspberry jam on top would add festive flair and a tangy, bright contrast to the wobbly cream base.

Serves 4

2 cups full-fat canned coconut milk, well-shaken

1 cup pumpkin purée

¼ cup maple syrup, plus more for serving

2 tablespoons packed demerara sugar (dark brown sugar)

1 tablespoon agar-agar flakes

2 teaspoons vanilla extract or paste or fresh vanilla bean seeds

½ teaspoon ground cinnamon or pumpkin spice (see page **247**), (optional; will taste more like pumpkin pie filling if added)

¼ teaspoon salt

roasted hazelnuts, chopped

In a large pot or high-sided skillet, whisk together all ingredients except hazelnuts. Whisking constantly, bring to gentle boil over medium heat. Continue to cook and whisk for 5 to 8 minutes until brown sugar and agar-agar have dissolved. Pour into ramekins or teacups and chill for at least 6 hours. Run a sharp knife around outside of set panna cotta to loosen seal, invert serving plate over cup, and flip to release panna cotta. You can serve them in the ramekins or cups if you prefer. Serve chilled with a drizzle of maple syrup and tumble of hazelnuts.

DULCE DE LECHE PUMPKIN MOUSSE

This thick, rich, quick-to-make mousse is for those with a serious sweet tooth and little time. I use jarred dulce de leche (look for a high-quality version with no preservatives, additives, or dyes) for a bit of a cheat. I like to dip buttery, melt-in-your-mouth shortbread cookies into this pumpkin caramel cloud pot, using them as an edible spoon (optional, but recommended).

.... *Serves 4–6* ....

½ cup heavy whipping cream
½ cup high-quality jarred dulce de leche or thick caramel, chilled
1 teaspoon vanilla extract
¼ teaspoon salt
1 cup pumpkin purée, chilled
Maple Pumpkin Spice Pumpkin Seeds (see page **252**) or chopped pecans

Add cream to a stand mixer fitted with a whisk attachment or a large bowl for a handheld mixer. Beat on high until stiff peaks form. Add dulce de leche or caramel, vanilla, and salt; briefly beat until combined. Add pumpkin and beat on high for 30 seconds to 1 minute, until blended and fluffy. Transfer mousse to serving cups and refrigerate for at least 1 hour, or until cold. Garnish with pumpkin seeds or pecans and serve.

EXTRAS

Including final touches required or suggested in several of this book's recipes, this chapter doesn't hog the spotlight, but offers a few recipe backbones more complex pumpkin creations would fall flat without. There are recipes in here that defy pumpkin's common fall and winter placement, feeling at home during spring and summer, too. From condiments to garnishes to crusts to simple roasted pumpkins and their seeds, these tiny addendums can be employed as instructed or in a new way altogether.

RECIPES

HOW TO COOK PUMPKIN

243

SPELT PIE CRUST

244

HOMEMADE PUMPKIN SPICE

247

PUMPKIN BUTTER

248

PUMPKIN SEED BUTTER

251

PUMPKIN SEED SAUCE

251

ROASTED PUMPKIN SEEDS WITH SWEET & SAVORY VARIATIONS

252

HOW TO COOK PUMPKIN

Directions for roasted pumpkin cubes and roasted pumpkin purée.

Roasted Pumpkin

For roasted pumpkin cubes

1 (2–3 pound) pumpkin, any variety, peeled, seeded, and cut into ½-inch pieces
1 tablespoon extra-virgin olive oil
salt, to taste

Preheat oven to 375ºF. On a large-rimmed baking sheet, toss pumpkin with oil and salt. Roast for 35 to 45 minutes, until tender and beginning to brown. Enjoy alone or add to any recipe that calls for cubed, roasted pumpkin.

For roasted pumpkin purée

Makes 2½ cups of purée (approximate amount from 1 (2–3 pound) pumpkin)

1 (2–3 pound) pumpkin, halved and seeded

Preheat oven to 375ºF. Line a large-rimmed baking sheet with parchment paper and place pumpkin cut-side down (skin faces up). Roast for 45 to 60 minutes, until collapsed and extremely tender when pierced with a knife. Cool until you can handle it comfortably.

To purée, scoop cooled pumpkin flesh into a food processor; discard skin. Blend until smooth and creamy, stopping to scrape down sides once or twice. Store in a zip-top bag in the freezer for up to 3 months (see *Notes*).

> **NOTES**
>
> Don't roast a Halloween carving pumpkin—they're watery, stringy, and lacking in flavor. Stick to buttercup, red kuri, turban, kabocha, jarrahdale, or other heirloom cooking varieties for roasted cubes and purées.
>
> While sugar pumpkin may seem like the obvious choice for pumpkin pie and desserts, I find it quite watery, stringy, and bland. I prefer jarrahdale, red kuri, buttercup, butternut, kabocha, or cheese pumpkin to sugar pumpkin for purée.
>
> For pumpkin purée, you can roast more than one pumpkin at a time, but only blend one pumpkin at a time in the food processor.
>
> Some types of pumpkin freeze better than others. Canned pumpkin does not freeze well, becoming separated and watery upon defrosting; ditto buttercup and kabocha purées. If you can, resist freezing plain purée (many recipes containing pumpkin purée freeze beautifully, though).

SPELT PIE CRUST

When I developed this pastry, I was surprised at how beautifully spelt—a whole grain—worked to create a tender, flaky, incredibly rich crust. It holds its shape in the oven and can be used for either sweet or savory pies, galettes, tarts, quiches, and turnovers—the sky is the limit with this versatile recipe. I like to make my pastry in a food processor for ease and to avoid heating the butter with my hands too much, but a pastry cutter and elbow grease will work, too.

Makes 2 (9–11-inch) pie crusts

3 cups light or dark spelt flour (both work very well; light will yield a more traditional look)

1 tablespoon evaporated cane sugar

½ teaspoon salt

1½ cups unsalted butter, cut into small cubes, very cold

⅓–½ cup ice water

In a food processor, pulse flour, sugar, and salt, or mix in a large bowl by hand. Add butter and pulse or cut in with a pastry cutter until a coarse meal forms and butter is barely visible. While pulsing or stirring with a wooden spoon, pour ice water through chute or directly into the bowl until a rough dough forms and mixture holds together when pressed between two fingers. Dump dough onto a clean countertop and shape into 2 (1-inch-high) discs. Wrap dough discs in plastic and chill until cold (about 1 hour). Roll and bake according to the specific recipe's instruction.

HOMEMADE PUMPKIN SPICE

If you've only ever purchased pre-mixed pumpkin spice, please give this a go—there's a surprisingly big difference in taste. And, for the amount we use during fall and winter, it's far more economical to boot. I purchase spices at a bulk food store for greater variety, value, and freshness (just make sure your store has a good turnover rate). Keep this addictive spice mix handy to perfectly season the holiday season. To be clear, there is no actual pumpkin in pumpkin spice.

Makes 1 large jarful

½ cup ground cinnamon
⅓ cup ground nutmeg
⅓ cup ground dried ginger
¼ cup ground allspice
3 tablespoons ground cloves

Add all ingredients to an airtight glass jar, seal, and shake until combined. Store in the pantry for up to 1 year.

PUMPKIN BUTTER

Pumpkin butter is my kryptonite, and if you're like me, you may even begin saying, "Yes, we can pumpkin butter that." It's the ultimate foil to both savory and sweet flavors (see *Serving Suggestions*), and it freezes perfectly, allowing you to save some for later.

Makes 3–4 cups

4 cups pumpkin purée
½ cup maple syrup or lightly packed light brown sugar
2 teaspoons pumpkin spice (see page **247**)
1 teaspoon apple cider vinegar
⅛ teaspoon salt

Mix all ingredients in a slow cooker. Set on low and cook for 6 hours, stirring once or twice throughout. Stir well, cool, and store airtight in the refrigerator for up to 1 month or freeze for up to 3 months.

SERVING SUGGESTIONS

Stir pumpkin butter into cooked oatmeal; spread on toast; stir into plain yogurt; use as a topping for ice cream; spread onto waffles or pancakes; use as a condiment on a cheese board or spicy curry; use alongside a sharp cheddar for grilled cheese sandwiches; spread on a muffin or bagel; blend into smoothies; and more.

PUMPKIN SEED BUTTER

For this recipe, only use store-bought green pumpkin seeds, not the ones from your jack-o-lantern.

2 cups raw, unsalted green pumpkin seeds
1 tablespoon pumpkin seed oil or extra-virgin olive oil

Preheat oven to 300°F. Spread seeds onto a large-rimmed baking sheet and roast for 20 minutes. Cool completely. Add to a food processor and blend for 5 minutes. Scrape down sides and add oil. Blend again until very creamy and the consistency of runny peanut butter. Transfer to a glass jar and store in refrigerator for up to 2 months. Stir well before using.

PUMPKIN SEED SAUCE

This is a creamy, dairy-free pumpkin seed sauce snagged from my first cookbook, *Whole Bowls*. I use the pastel green condiment for tacos, warm brown rice, bowls (obviously), hearty salads, roasted vegetables, and as a dip for crudités.

½ cup plus 2 tablespoons very hot, recently boiled water
⅓ cup raw, unsalted green pumpkin seeds
1 clove garlic, minced
2 tablespoons lime juice
1 tablespoon maple syrup
1 tablespoon pumpkin seed oil or extra-virgin olive oil
1 teaspoon ground cumin
½ teaspoon sea salt

Add all sauce ingredients to a blender and blend until smooth. Store in a glass jar or airtight container in refrigerator for up to 4 days; shake or stir before using.

ROASTED PUMPKIN SEEDS WITH SWEET & SAVORY VARIATIONS

A crunchy, high protein snack, roasted pumpkin seeds do the heavy lifting anywhere you need a touch of crunch. Sprinkle on soups, salads, trail mix, yogurt, ice cream, pie, or simply enjoy by the handful, it's hard to go wrong with this seasonal treat.

.... *Makes ½ cup (seeds from 1 sugar pumpkin)* ....

Maple Pumpkin Spice Pumpkin Seeds

½ cup fresh pumpkin seeds, cleaned and dried well, or raw, unsalted green pumpkin seeds
1 tablespoon maple syrup
½ teaspoon pumpkin spice (see page **247**)
⅛ teaspoon salt

Preheat oven to 375°F. Line a large-rimmed baking sheet with parchment paper. Add all ingredients to baking sheet, tossing well to combine. Spread into a single layer. Roast for 25 to 30 minutes if using sugar pumpkin seeds or 10 to 15 minutes if using green pumpkin seeds, until brown and beginning to pop. Cool completely; maple syrup crisps as it cools. Store airtight at room temperature for up to 1 week.

Smoky Roasted Pumpkin Seeds

½ cup fresh pumpkin seeds, cleaned and dried well, or raw, unsalted green pumpkin seeds
1 teaspoon smoked paprika (mild or hot)
½ teaspoon extra-virgin olive oil
⅛ teaspoon salt

Preheat oven to 375°F. Line a large-rimmed baking sheet with parchment paper. Add all ingredients to baking sheet, tossing well to combine. Spread into a single layer. Roast for 25 to 30 minutes if using sugar pumpkin seeds or 10 to 15 minutes if using green pumpkin seeds, until brown and beginning to pop. Cool completely. Store airtight at room temperature for up to 1 week.

ACKNOWLEDGMENTS

To my editor at Skyhorse Publishing, Nicole Frail, thank you for making *Purely Pumpkin* a possibility, and for giving me all of the creative freedom I could ask for. To my literary agent, Carly Watters, thank you for getting me to the front of the line to write this and for your continuing career guidance in the world of publishing. Nicole and Carly, working together on two cookbooks in two years has been a true delight and a testament to the power of teamwork.

To my family: Dad, Kirsten, Stewart, Katie, Chloe, Ava, and Ryan, thank you for your enduring support.

To Geoff Woodley, a man with very distinct, high-rent taste in beverages, thank you for helping me "research" (drink) pumpkin spice lattés so I'd have something to work with—I know you lost a bit of your cachet that evening. And, for your gorgeous latté art and beverage styling on several of the recipes, working with me over a couple of afternoons at the Detour Coffee roastery (detourcoffee.com) so I could get the perfect shot for these pages—thank you! You are not malarkey. (Hey, Santa.)

I've been astounded by the generosity of the many farmers and producers in Ontario, Canada, and beyond. Thank you for informing me of the seemingly endless, always delicious varieties of pumpkin and squash available right in my backyard. It's been a pleasure getting to know some of you through your work, and I've been further convinced that local food is the tastiest food.

Last but not least, a big hug, high-five, and thank you to all the readers of my blog, *Yummy Beet*. Your excitement about vegetables and acceptance of my enthusiasm for produce makes me bounce out of bed in the morning. I'm looking forward to sharing more stories, recipes, and photographs for years to come.

INDEX

A

Agar-agar flakes
Vegan Coconut, Vanilla Bean, and Pumpkin
Panna Cotta, 234

Allspice
Homemade Pumpkin Spice, 247

Almonds
Black Quinoa with Heirloom Pumpkin,
Chestnuts, and Mint, 135
Brown Butter and Saffron Whole Wheat
Pumpkin Custard Cake, 215

American Tonda, 5

Anise
Pho with Pumpkin, Spelt Noodles, Mushrooms,
and Tofu, 90

Apple and Cheese Melts with Pumpkin Ketchup,
162

Apples
Apple and Cheese Melts with Pumpkin Ketchup,
162
Kale Slaw with Apples, White Cheddar, and
Pumpkin Honey Mustard Dressing, 131
Morning Glory Pumpkin Muffins, 81
Super-Seed Pumpkin Spice and Apple Muesli,
60
Twice-Baked Mashed Pumpkin and Apples with
Pecan Oat Crunch, 146

Arugula
Delicata Squash and Arugula Salad with
Pumpkin Seed Oil Vinaigrette, 128
Savory Herbed Pumpkin Oatmeal with Soft-
Boiled Eggs and Pumpkin Seed Pesto, 56

Avocado
Avocado Toast with Pumpkin Butter and
Sprouts, 68
Huevos Rancheros with Smoky Pumpkin Sauce,
75
Maple Roasted Pumpkin Crostini with Avocado,
Feta, and Balsamic Glaze, 103
Vegetable Brown Rice Sushi with Ginger
Pumpkin Dipping Sauce, 108

Avocado Toast with Pumpkin Butter and Sprouts,
68

B

Balsamic vinegar
Maple Roasted Pumpkin Crostini with Avocado,
Feta, and Balsamic Glaze, 103
Mushrooms and Kale Over Pumpkin Polenta,
187
Roasted Jarrahdale Pumpkin and Onions with
Lemony Whipped Feta, 132
Warm Wild Rice with Spinach, Pumpkin, and
Grapes, 142

Bananas
Morning Glory Pumpkin Muffins, 81
Pumpkin Pie Green Protein Smoothie, 43
Pumpkin Spice Smoothie Bowl, 40

Barley
Wild Mushroom and Pumpkin Barley Pesto, 168

Bean and Red Lentil Pumpkin Chili with Zucchini, 167

Beans
black
Bean and Red Lentil Pumpkin Chili with
Zucchini, 167
Huevos Rancheros with Smoky Pumpkin
Sauce, 75
white
Grain Bowls with Apple Cider Vinegar-
Roasted Pumpkin and Kimchi, 164

Vegan Pumpkin, Onion, and Spinach
Lasagna with White Bean Ricotta, 195
Béchamel
Lasagna with Pumpkin Orange Béchamel and
Ricotta Parmesan Béchamel, 191
Bell peppers
Shakshuka with Pumpkin and Peppers, 63
Beverages, 15–49
Black Futsu, 5
Black Pasta with Roasted Pumpkin and Chili, 173
Black Quinoa with Heirloom Pumpkin, Chestnuts,
and Mint, 135
Blue Doll, 5
Bok choy
Firecracker Stir-Fried Pumpkin, Bok Choy, and
Cashews, 188
Thai Coconut Soup with Pumpkin, Noodles,
and Lime, 95
Bourbon
Pumpkin Spiked Latté with Orange Peel, 31
Bread
Apple and Cheese Melts with Pumpkin Ketchup,
162
Avocado Toast with Pumpkin Butter and
Sprouts, 68
Easy Whole Wheat Pumpkin Flatbreads with
Lemon Thyme, 117
Maple Roasted Pumpkin Crostini with Avocado,
Feta, and Balsamic Glaze, 103
No-Knead Pumpkin Breakfast Braids, 77
Pumpkin Ginger Bread with Dark Chocolate
and Coconut, 78
Pumpkin Veggie Burgers with Halloumi and
Avocado, 171
Toast with Pumpkin, Kale, Mushrooms,
Poached Eggs, and Herb Oil, 73
Breakfast, 51–82
Broccoli rabe
Rapini and Roasted Garlic Pumpkin Galette
with Rosemary Spelt Crust, 174
Brown Butter and Saffron Whole Wheat Pumpkin
Custard Cake, 215
Brunch, 51–82
Brussels sprouts
Lemony Roasted Brussels Sprouts and Pumpkin
Seeds, 148

Silky Pumpkin Pasta with Roasted Brussels
Sprouts and Crispy Leaves, 183
Socca Pizza with Roasted Squash, Brussels
Sprouts, and Lemon, 191
Butter, pumpkin
Pumpkin Butter Pumpkin Spice Latté, 27
Buttercup, 5
Buttermilk
Super-Seed Pumpkin Spice and Apple Muesli, 60
Butternut, 7

C
Cake
Brown Butter and Saffron Whole Wheat
Pumpkin Custard Cake, 215
Calzone
Curried Pumpkin Tofu Calzones, 196
Caramel
Dulce de Leche Pumpkin Mousse, 237
Caraway
Shakshuka with Pumpkin and Peppers, 63
Cardamom
Honeyed Pumpkin Spice Masala Chai, 47
Pumpkin Cardamom Donuts with Chai Glaze,
225
Cashews
Firecracker Stir-Fried Pumpkin, Bok Choy, and
Cashews, 188
Vegan Pumpkin Eggnog, 44
Cheese
Apple and Cheese Melts with Pumpkin Ketchup,
162
cheddar
Kale Slaw with Apples, White Cheddar,
and Pumpkin Honey Mustard Dressing,
131
Sharp Cheddar, Pumpkin, and Pecan
Scones, 82
feta
Maple Roasted Pumpkin Crostini with
Avocado, Feta, and Balsamic Glaze, 103
Roasted Jarrahdale Pumpkin and Onions
with Lemony Whipped Feta, 132
goat
Pizza with Pumpkin, Goat Cheese, and
Kale, 159

gorgonzola
    Italian Pumpkin Holiday Salad with Gorgonzola and Cranberry Dressing, 127
parmesan
    Lasagna with Pumpkin Orange Béchamel and Ricotta Parmesan Béchamel, 191
ricotta
    Lasagna with Pumpkin Orange Béchamel and Ricotta Parmesan Béchamel, 191
Cherry jam
    Pumpkin Seed Oil Shortbread Jam Squares, 207
Chestnut jam
    Pumpkin Spice Rugelach with Chestnut Jam, 218
Chestnuts
    Black Quinoa with Heirloom Pumpkin, Chestnuts, and Mint, 135
    Mini Classic Pumpkin Pies, 204
Chia seeds
    Super-Seed Pumpkin Spice and Apple Muesli, 60
Chickpeas
    Moroccan Chickpea, Pumpkin, and Prune Stew, 184
    Pumpkin Veggie Burgers with Halloumi and Avocado, 171
    Roasted Garlic Pumpkin Hummus, 107
Chili
    Black Pasta with Roasted Pumpkin and Chili, 173
    Curried Pumpkin Tofu Calzones, 196
    Firecracker Stir-Fried Pumpkin, Bok Choy, and Cashews, 188
    Savory Yogurt with Roasted Pumpkin, Black Quinoa, Pumpkin Seed Pesto, and Chili, 71
    Thai Coconut Soup with Pumpkin, Noodles, and Lime, 95
Chili flakes
    Bean and Red Lentil Pumpkin Chili with Zucchini, 167
    Huevos Rancheros with Smoky Pumpkin Sauce, 75
    Moroccan Chickpea, Pumpkin, and Prune Stew, 184
    Pho with Pumpkin, Spelt Noodles, Mushrooms, and Tofu, 90

Poppy Seed Pumpkin and Mango Salad Rolls, 111
    Shakshuka with Pumpkin and Peppers, 63
    Vegetable Brown Rice Sushi with Ginger Pumpkin Dipping Sauce, 108
Chocolate
    Chocolate Pumpkin Seed Butter Cups, 211
    Cookies of Plenty with Chocolate, Pumpkin, Cranberries, and Pumpkin Seeds, 208
    Fudgy Pumpkin Coffee Brownies, 222
    Mini Classic Pumpkin Pies, 204
    Pumpkin Ginger Bread with Dark Chocolate and Coconut, 78
    Pumpkin Spice Hot Chocolate, 32
Chocolate Pumpkin Seed Butter Cups, 211
Cilantro
    Avocado Toast with Pumpkin Butter and Sprouts, 68
    Curried Pumpkin Tofu Calzones, 196
    Halloumi Pumpkin Parcels with Pomegranate and Black Sesame, 103
    Honeyed Pumpkin, Fig, and Tahini Bites, 113
    Lettuce Cups with Orange, Cumin Seed Roasted Pumpkin and Tahini Yogurt Dressing, 124
    Pho with Pumpkin, Spelt Noodles, Mushrooms, and Tofu, 90
    Poppy Seed Pumpkin and Mango Salad Rolls, 111
    Pumpkin Veggie Burgers with Halloumi and Avocado, 171
    Vegetable Brown Rice Sushi with Ginger Pumpkin Dipping Sauce, 108
Cinderella, 5
Cinnamon
    Homemade Pumpkin Spice, 247
    Morning Glory Pumpkin Muffins, 81
    Moroccan Chickpea, Pumpkin, and Prune Stew, 184
    Pumpkin Cardamom Donuts with Chai Glaze, 225
    Vanilla Roasted Pumpkin Wedges, 145
    Vegan Coconut, Vanilla Bean, and Pumpkin Panna Cotta, 234
Classic Pumpkin Pie, 203
Classic Pumpkin Spice Latté, 24
Clementines

Silky Pumpkin Ginger Soup with Clementine and Vanilla, 96
Skillet Pumpkin with Brown Butter, Honey, and Clementine, 139
Cloves
Apple and Cheese Melts with Pumpkin Ketchup, 162
Homemade Pumpkin Spice, 247
Pumpkin Cardamom Donuts with Chai Glaze, 225
Vegan Pumpkin, Onion, and Spinach Lasagna with White Bean Ricotta, 195
Cocoa powder
Pumpkin Spice Hot Chocolate, 32
Coconut
Pumpkin Ginger Bread with Dark Chocolate and Coconut, 78
Thai Coconut Soup with Pumpkin, Noodles, and Lime, 95
Coconut milk
Black Quinoa with Heirloom Pumpkin, Chestnuts, and Mint, 135
Gingerbread Pumpkin and Hazelnut Shake, 39
Thai Coconut Soup with Pumpkin, Noodles, and Lime, 95
Twice-Baked Mashed Pumpkin and Apples with Pecan Oat Crunch, 146
Vegan Coconut, Vanilla Bean, and Pumpkin Panna Cotta, 234
Coconut oil
Curried Pumpkin Tofu Calzones, 196
Firecracker Stir-Fried Pumpkin, Bok Choy, and Cashews, 188
Grain Bowls with Apple Cider Vinegar-Roasted Pumpkin and Kimchi, 164
Poppy Seed Pumpkin and Mango Salad Rolls, 111
Pumpkin Cardamom Donuts with Chai Glaze, 225
Pumpkin Pie Granola with Pecans, 59
Thai Coconut Soup with Pumpkin, Noodles, and Lime, 95
Coffee
Classic Pumpkin Spice Latté, 24
Fudgy Pumpkin Coffee Brownies, 222
Pumpkin Butter Pumpkin Spice Latté, 27
Pumpkin Spiked Latté with Orange Peel, 31
Salted Caramel Pumpkin Spice Latté, 28
Cookies of Plenty with Chocolate, Pumpkin, Cranberries, and Pumpkin Seeds, 208
Cornucopia-Stuffed Pumpkin, 160
Couscous
Moroccan Chickpea, Pumpkin, and Prune Stew, 184
Cranberries
Cookies of Plenty with Chocolate, Pumpkin, Cranberries, and Pumpkin Seeds, 208
Cornucopia-Stuffed Pumpkin, 160
Cranberry-Pumpkin Clafoutis with Oat Flour, 230
Delicata Squash and Arugula Salad with Pumpkin Seed Oil Vinaigrette, 128
Italian Pumpkin Holiday Salad with Gorgonzola and Cranberry Dressing, 127
Cranberry-Pumpkin Clafoutis with Oat Flour, 230
Cream cheese
Gingerbread Pumpkin Cheesecake with Pecan Oat Crust, 213
Pumpkin Spice Rugelach with Chestnut Jam, 218
Crème brûlée, 233
Croutons
Pumpkin Caesar Salad with Sage Sourdough Croutons, 123
Cucumber
Vegetable Brown Rice Sushi with Ginger Pumpkin Dipping Sauce, 108
Cumin
Bean and Red Lentil Pumpkin Chili with Zucchini, 167
Halloumi Pumpkin Parcels with Pomegranate and Black Sesame, 103
Huevos Rancheros with Smoky Pumpkin Sauce, 75
Lettuce Cups with Orange, Cumin Seed Roasted Pumpkin and Tahini Yogurt Dressing, 124
Millet Couscous with Roasted Parsnips, Pumpkin, and Mint, 140
Moroccan Chickpea, Pumpkin, and Prune Stew, 184
Pumpkin Seed Sauce, 251
Roasted Garlic Pumpkin Hummus, 107

Shakshuka with Pumpkin and Peppers, 63
Curried Pumpkin Tofu Calzones, 196
Curry powder
    Curried Pumpkin Tofu Calzones, 196

D
Dates
    Pumpkin Seed "Nut" Milk, 49
    Sticky Toffee Pumpkin Spice Pecan Truffles, 217
Delicata Squash and Arugula Salad with Pumpkin
    Seed Oil Vinaigrette, 128
Deserts, 199–237
Donuts
    Pumpkin Cardamom Donuts with Chai Glaze,
    225
Dulce de Leche Pumpkin Mousse, 237

E
Easy Lentil Soup with Greens and Pumpkin, 93
Easy Whole Wheat Pumpkin Flatbreads with
    Lemon Thyme, 117
Eggnog, 44
Eggplant
    Thai Coconut Soup with Pumpkin, Noodles,
    and Lime, 95
Eggs
    Huevos Rancheros with Smoky Pumpkin Sauce,
    75
    Pumpkin Deviled Eggs with Maple Pecan
    "Bacon," 114
Espresso
    Classic Pumpkin Spice Latté, 24
    Pumpkin Butter Pumpkin Spice Latté, 27
    Pumpkin Spiked Latté with Orange Peel, 31
    Salted Caramel Pumpkin Spice Latté, 28

F
Fairytale, 7
Figs
    Honeyed Pumpkin, Fig, and Tahini Bites, 113
Firecracker Stir-Fried Pumpkin, Bok Choy, and
    Cashews, 188
Flatbread
    Easy Whole Wheat Pumpkin Flatbreads with
    Lemon Thyme, 117
Flat White Boer, 7

Flesh. *See* Pumpkin flesh
French Turban, 11
Fudgy Pumpkin Coffee Brownies, 222

G
Galeux d'Eysines, 7
Garam masala
    Curried Pumpkin Tofu Calzones, 196
    Mellow Meyer Lemon Pumpkin Curry Bowls,
    177
Ginger
    Gingerbread Pumpkin and Hazelnut Shake, 39
    Gingerbread Pumpkin Cheesecake with Pecan
    Oat Crust, 213
    Homemade Pumpkin Spice, 247
    Honeyed Pumpkin Spice Masala Chai, 47
    Matcha Pumpkin Latté with Orange Peel with
    Ginger and Orange Flower Water, 36
    Pho with Pumpkin, Spelt Noodles, Mushrooms,
    and Tofu, 90
    Pumpkin Cardamom Donuts with Chai Glaze,
    225
    Roasted Garlic Pumpkin Hummus, 107
    Salted Honey Pumpkin Crème Brûlée, 233
    Silky Pumpkin Ginger Soup with Clementine
    and Vanilla, 96
    Spelt Pumpkin Spice Gingerbread Forest
    Animal Cookies, 227–228
    Vegetable Brown Rice Sushi with Ginger
    Pumpkin Dipping Sauce, 108
Ginger bread
    Pumpkin Ginger Bread with Dark Chocolate
    and Coconut, 78
Gingerbread Pumpkin and Hazelnut Shake, 39
Gingerbread Pumpkin Cheesecake with Pecan Oat
    Crust, 213
Gluten-Free Pumpkin Sour Cream Pancakes, 64
Gnocchi
    Heirloom Pumpkin Gnocchi with Mint and
    Garlic, 179
    Heirloom Pumpkin Gnocchi with Oven-
    Roasted Tomato Sauce, 180
Grain Bowls with Apple Cider Vinegar-Roasted
    Pumpkin and Kimchi, 164
Granola, 59
Grapes

Warm Wild Rice with Spinach, Pumpkin, and
	Grapes, 142
Greek yogurt
	Heirloom Pumpkin Gnocchi with Mint and
		Garlic, 179
	Mini Classic Pumpkin Pies, 204
	Pumpkin Spice Smoothie Bowl, 40
Greens
	Easy Lentil Soup with Greens and Pumpkin, 93

H
Halloumi
	Pumpkin Veggie Burgers with Halloumi and
		Avocado, 171
Halloumi Pumpkin Parcels with Pomegranate and
	Black Sesame, 103
Hazelnuts
	Gingerbread Pumpkin and Hazelnut Shake, 39
	Vegan Coconut, Vanilla Bean, and Pumpkin
		Panna Cotta, 234
Heirloom Butternut, 7
Heirloom Pumpkin Gnocchi with Mint and Garlic,
	179
Heirloom Pumpkin Gnocchi with Oven-Roasted
	Tomato Sauce, 180
Heirloom pumpkins, 5–11
Hemp seeds
	Super-Seed Pumpkin Spice and Apple Muesli,
		60
Homemade Pumpkin Butter Poptarts, 221
Honey
	Apple and Cheese Melts with Pumpkin Ketchup,
		162
	Black Pasta with Roasted Pumpkin and Chili,
		173
	Black Quinoa with Heirloom Pumpkin,
		Chestnuts, and Mint, 135
	Firecracker Stir-Fried Pumpkin, Bok Choy, and
		Cashews, 188
	Honeyed Pumpkin, Fig, and Tahini Bites, 113
	Honeyed Pumpkin Spice Masala Chai, 47
	Italian Pumpkin Holiday Salad with Gorgonzola
		and Cranberry Dressing, 127
	Kale Slaw with Apples, White Cheddar, and
		Pumpkin Honey Mustard Dressing, 131
	Matcha Pumpkin Latté with Orange Peel with

	Ginger and Orange Flower Water, 36
	Salted Honey Pumpkin Crème Brûlée, 233
	Skillet Pumpkin with Brown Butter, Honey, and
		Clementine, 139
	Vegetable Brown Rice Sushi with Ginger
		Pumpkin Dipping Sauce, 108
Honeyed Pumpkin, Fig, and Tahini Bites, 113
Honeyed Pumpkin Spice Masala Chai, 47
Hooligan, 7
Hubbard, 7
Huevos Rancheros with Smoky Pumpkin Sauce, 75
Hummus
	Roasted Garlic Pumpkin Hummus, 107

I
Italian Pumpkin Holiday Salad with Gorgonzola
	and Cranberry Dressing, 127

J
Jalapeño
	Huevos Rancheros with Smoky Pumpkin Sauce,
		75
Jam
	Pumpkin Seed Oil Shortbread Jam Squares, 207
	Pumpkin Spice Rugelach with Chestnut Jam,
		218
Japanese eggplant
	Thai Coconut Soup with Pumpkin, Noodles,
		and Lime, 95
Jarrahdale, 7

K
Kabocha, 7
Kale
	Easy Lentil Soup with Greens and Pumpkin, 93
	Kale Slaw with Apples, White Cheddar, and
		Pumpkin Honey Mustard Dressing, 131
	Mushrooms and Kale Over Pumpkin Polenta,
		187
	Pizza with Pumpkin, Goat Cheese, and Kale,
		159
	Pumpkin Veggie Burgers with Halloumi and
		Avocado, 171
	Toast with Pumpkin, Kale, Mushrooms,
		Poached Eggs, and Herb Oil, 73
Kale Slaw with Apples, White Cheddar, and

Pumpkin Honey Mustard Dressing, 131

Kefir
Super-Seed Pumpkin Spice and Apple Muesli, 60

Ketchup
Apple and Cheese Melts with Pumpkin Ketchup, 162

Kimchi
Grain Bowls with Apple Cider Vinegar-Roasted Pumpkin and Kimchi, 164

L

Lasagna
Vegan Pumpkin, Onion, and Spinach Lasagna with White Bean Ricotta, 195

Lasagna with Pumpkin Orange Béchamel and Ricotta Parmesan Béchamel, 191

Latté
base, 23
Classic Pumpkin Spice Latté, 24
Pumpkin Butter Pumpkin Spice Latté, 27
Salted Caramel Pumpkin Spice Latté, 28

Lemon
Easy Whole Wheat Pumpkin Flatbreads with Lemon Thyme, 117
Mellow Meyer Lemon Pumpkin Curry Bowls, 177
Roasted Jarrahdale Pumpkin and Onions with Lemony Whipped Feta, 132
Socca Pizza with Roasted Squash, Brussels Sprouts, and Lemon, 191

Lemony Roasted Brussels Sprouts and Pumpkin Seeds, 148

Lentils
Bean and Red Lentil Pumpkin Chili with Zucchini, 167
Easy Lentil Soup with Greens and Pumpkin, 93

Lettuce
Italian Pumpkin Holiday Salad with Gorgonzola and Cranberry Dressing, 127
Poppy Seed Pumpkin and Mango Salad Rolls, 111
Pumpkin Caesar Salad with Sage Sourdough Croutons, 123
Pumpkin Veggie Burgers with Halloumi and Avocado, 171

Lettuce Cups with Orange, Cumin Seed Roasted

Pumpkin and Tahini Yogurt Dressing, 124

Lime
Huevos Rancheros with Smoky Pumpkin Sauce, 75
Thai Coconut Soup with Pumpkin, Noodles, and Lime, 95

Linguine
Thai Coconut Soup with Pumpkin, Noodles, and Lime, 95

Long Island Cheese, 7

M

Mains, 153–196

Mango
Poppy Seed Pumpkin and Mango Salad Rolls, 111

Maple Pumpkin Spice Pumpkin Seeds, 252

Maple Roasted Pumpkin Crostini with Avocado, Feta, and Balsamic Glaze, 103

Maple syrup
Chocolate Pumpkin Seed Butter Cups, 211
Delicata Squash and Arugula Salad with Pumpkin Seed Oil Vinaigrette, 128
Gingerbread Pumpkin and Hazelnut Shake, 39
Homemade Pumpkin Spice, 251
Maple Pumpkin Spice Pumpkin Seeds, 252
Maple Roasted Pumpkin Crostini with Avocado, Feta, and Balsamic Glaze, 103
Mini Classic Pumpkin Pies, 204
Pho with Pumpkin, Spelt Noodles, Mushrooms, and Tofu, 90
Pumpkin Butter, 248
Pumpkin Deviled Eggs with Maple Pecan "Bacon," 114
Pumpkin Pie Granola with Pecans, 59
Pumpkin Pie Green Protein Smoothie, 43
Pumpkin Spice Smoothie Bowl, 40
Roasted Garlic Pumpkin Hummus, 107
Super-Seed Pumpkin Spice and Apple Muesli, 60
Vegan Coconut, Vanilla Bean, and Pumpkin Panna Cotta, 234
Vegan Pumpkin Eggnog, 44
Wild Rice and Oat Flourless Pumpkin Pancakes, 67

Marina di Chioggia, 8

Matcha powder
    Matcha Pumpkin Latté with Orange Peel with
        Ginger and Orange Flower Water, 36
Matcha Pumpkin Latté with Orange Peel with
    Ginger and Orange Flower Water, 36
Mayonnaise
    Pumpkin Deviled Eggs with Maple Pecan
        "Bacon," 114
Mellow Meyer Lemon Pumpkin Curry Bowls, 177
Meringue
    Spelt Pumpkin Spice Gingerbread Forest
        Animal Cookies, 227–228
Milk
    Classic Pumpkin Spice Latté, 24
    Cranberry-Pumpkin Clafoutis with Oat Flour,
        230
    Gingerbread Pumpkin and Hazelnut Shake, 39
    Gluten-Free Pumpkin Sour Cream Pancakes, 64
    Homemade Pumpkin Butter Poptarts, 221
    Honeyed Pumpkin Spice Masala Chai, 47
    Lasagna with Pumpkin Orange Béchamel and
        Ricotta Parmesan Béchamel, 191
    Matcha Pumpkin Latté with Orange Peel with
        Ginger and Orange Flower Water, 36
    No-Knead Pumpkin Breakfast Braids, 77
    Pumpkin Butter Pumpkin Spice Latté, 27
    Pumpkin Ginger Bread with Dark Chocolate
        and Coconut, 78
    Pumpkin Pie Green Protein Smoothie, 43
    Pumpkin Spice Hot Chocolate, 32
    Pumpkin Spiked Latté with Orange Peel, 31
    Salted Caramel Pumpkin Spice Latté, 28
    Savory Herbed Pumpkin Oatmeal with Soft-
        Boiled Eggs and Pumpkin Seed Pesto, 56
    Spiced Pumpkin Oatmeal with Baked Pears and
        Pecans, 55
Millet Couscous with Roasted Parsnips, Pumpkin,
    and Mint, 140
Mini Classic Pumpkin Pies, 204
Mint
    Black Quinoa with Heirloom Pumpkin,
        Chestnuts, and Mint, 135
    Halloumi Pumpkin Parcels with Pomegranate
        and Black Sesame, 103
    Heirloom Pumpkin Gnocchi with Mint and
        Garlic, 179

Honeyed Pumpkin, Fig, and Tahini Bites, 113
Lettuce Cups with Orange, Cumin Seed Roasted
    Pumpkin and Tahini Yogurt Dressing, 124
Millet Couscous with Roasted Parsnips,
    Pumpkin, and Mint, 140
Miso
    Pho with Pumpkin, Spelt Noodles, Mushrooms,
        and Tofu, 90
    Vegetable Brown Rice Sushi with Ginger
        Pumpkin Dipping Sauce, 108
Molasses
    Gingerbread Pumpkin and Hazelnut Shake, 39
    Gingerbread Pumpkin Cheesecake with Pecan
        Oat Crust, 213
    Pumpkin Ginger Bread with Dark Chocolate
        and Coconut, 78
    Spelt Pumpkin Spice Gingerbread Forest
        Animal Cookies, 227–228
Morning Glory Pumpkin Muffins, 81
Moroccan Chickpea, Pumpkin, and Prune Stew,
    184
Muesli, 60
Muffins
    Morning Glory Pumpkin Muffins, 81
Mushrooms
    Cornucopia-Stuffed Pumpkin, 160
    Mushrooms and Kale Over Pumpkin Polenta,
        187
    Pho with Pumpkin, Spelt Noodles, Mushrooms,
        and Tofu, 90
    Toast with Pumpkin, Kale, Mushrooms,
        Poached Eggs, and Herb Oil, 73
    Wild Mushroom and Pumpkin Barley Pesto, 168
Mushrooms and Kale Over Pumpkin Polenta, 187
Musquée de Provence, 7
Mustard
    Delicata Squash and Arugula Salad with
        Pumpkin Seed Oil Vinaigrette, 128
    Kale Slaw with Apples, White Cheddar, and
        Pumpkin Honey Mustard Dressing, 131

N
No-Knead Pumpkin Breakfast Braids, 77
Nori
    Vegetable Brown Rice Sushi with Ginger
        Pumpkin Dipping Sauce, 108

Nutmeg
   Homemade Pumpkin Spice, 247
   Lasagna with Pumpkin Orange Béchamel and
      Ricotta Parmesan Béchamel, 191
   Pumpkin Ginger Bread with Dark Chocolate
      and Coconut, 78
   Rapini and Roasted Garlic Pumpkin Galette
      with Rosemary Spelt Crust, 174
   Salted Honey Pumpkin Crème Brûlée, 233
   Sharp Cheddar, Pumpkin, and Pecan Scones, 82
   Silky Pumpkin Pasta with Roasted Brussels
      Sprouts and Crispy Leaves, 183
   Vegan Pumpkin Eggnog, 44
   Wild Rice and Oat Flourless Pumpkin Pancakes,
      67
Nutrition, 13

O

Oats
   Cookies of Plenty with Chocolate, Pumpkin,
      Cranberries, and Pumpkin Seeds, 208
   Gingerbread Pumpkin Cheesecake with Pecan
      Oat Crust, 213
   Pumpkin Veggie Burgers with Halloumi and
      Avocado, 171
   Savory Herbed Pumpkin Oatmeal with Soft-
      Boiled Eggs and Pumpkin Seed Pesto, 56
   Spiced Pumpkin Oatmeal with Baked Pears and
      Pecans, 55
   Super-Seed Pumpkin Spice and Apple Muesli,
      60
   Twice-Baked Mashed Pumpkin and Apples with
      Pecan Oat Crunch, 146
   Wild Rice and Oat Flourless Pumpkin Pancakes,
      67
Olives
   Italian Pumpkin Holiday Salad with Gorgonzola
      and Cranberry Dressing, 127
One Too Many, 8
Orange flower water
   Matcha Pumpkin Latté with Orange Peel with
      Ginger and Orange Flower Water, 36
Orange Hokkaido, 8
Orange peel
   Pumpkin Spiked Latté with Orange Peel, 31
Oranges

Lettuce Cups with Orange, Cumin Seed Roasted
      Pumpkin and Tahini Yogurt Dressing, 124
Oregano
   Bean and Red Lentil Pumpkin Chili with
      Zucchini, 167
   Lasagna with Pumpkin Orange Béchamel and
      Ricotta Parmesan Béchamel, 191

P

Pancakes
   Gluten-Free Pumpkin Sour Cream Pancakes, 64
Paprika
   Bean and Red Lentil Pumpkin Chili with
      Zucchini, 167
   Huevos Rancheros with Smoky Pumpkin Sauce,
      75
   Pumpkin Deviled Eggs with Maple Pecan
      "Bacon," 114
   Shakshuka with Pumpkin and Peppers, 63
   Silky Pumpkin Pasta with Roasted Brussels
      Sprouts and Crispy Leaves, 183
Parsley
   Cornucopia-Stuffed Pumpkin, 160
   Pumpkin Veggie Burgers with Halloumi and
      Avocado, 171
Parsnips
   Millet Couscous with Roasted Parsnips,
      Pumpkin, and Mint, 140
Pasta
   Black Pasta with Roasted Pumpkin and Chili,
      173
   Heirloom Pumpkin Gnocchi with Mint and
      Garlic, 179
   Heirloom Pumpkin Gnocchi with Oven-
      Roasted Tomato Sauce, 180
   Pho with Pumpkin, Spelt Noodles, Mushrooms,
      and Tofu, 90
   Silky Pumpkin Pasta with Roasted Brussels
      Sprouts and Crispy Leaves, 183
   Thai Coconut Soup with Pumpkin, Noodles,
      and Lime, 95
   Vegan Pumpkin, Onion, and Spinach Lasagna
      with White Bean Ricotta, 195
Pearl barley
   Wild Mushroom and Pumpkin Barley Pesto, 168
Pears

Spiced Pumpkin Oatmeal with Baked Pears and
Pecans, 55
Pea sprouts
Bean and Red Lentil Pumpkin Chili with
Zucchini, 167
Pecans
Delicata Squash and Arugula Salad with
Pumpkin Seed Oil Vinaigrette, 128
Gingerbread Pumpkin Cheesecake with Pecan
Oat Crust, 213
Mini Classic Pumpkin Pies, 204
Pumpkin Deviled Eggs with Maple Pecan
"Bacon," 114
Pumpkin Pie Granola with Pecans, 59
Sharp Cheddar, Pumpkin, and Pecan Scones, 82
Spiced Pumpkin Oatmeal with Baked Pears and
Pecans, 55
Sticky Toffee Pumpkin Spice Pecan Truffles, 217
Twice-Baked Mashed Pumpkin and Apples with
Pecan Oat Crunch, 146
Pesto
Savory Herbed Pumpkin Oatmeal with Soft-
Boiled Eggs and Pumpkin Seed Pesto, 56
Savory Yogurt with Roasted Pumpkin, Black
Quinoa, Pumpkin Seed Pesto, and Chili, 71
Socca Pizza with Roasted Squash, Brussels
Sprouts, and Lemon, 191
Pho with Pumpkin, Spelt Noodles, Mushrooms,
and Tofu, 90
Pie
Classic Pumpkin Pie, 203
Mini Classic Pumpkin Pies, 204
Spelt Pie Crust, 244
Pink Banana, 8
Pistachios
Brown Butter and Saffron Whole Wheat
Pumpkin Custard Cake, 215
Pizza
Socca Pizza with Roasted Squash, Brussels
Sprouts, and Lemon, 191
Pizza with Pumpkin, Goat Cheese, and Kale, 159
Polenta
Mushrooms and Kale Over Pumpkin Polenta, 187
Pomegranate
Halloumi Pumpkin Parcels with Pomegranate
and Black Sesame, 103

Roasted Pumpkin with Onions, Pomegranate
and Yogurt, 136
Super-Seed Pumpkin Spice and Apple Muesli,
60
Poppy seed
Morning Glory Pumpkin Muffins, 81
Poppy Seed Pumpkin and Mango Salad Rolls,
111
Roasted Garlic Pumpkin Hummus, 107
Poppy Seed Pumpkin and Mango Salad Rolls, 111
Porcelain Doll, 8
Prunes
Moroccan Chickpea, Pumpkin, and Prune Stew,
184
Pumpkin butter, 248
Avocado Toast with Pumpkin Butter and
Sprouts, 68
Homemade Pumpkin Butter Poptarts, 221
Pumpkin Butter Pumpkin Spice Latté, 27
Toast with Pumpkin, Kale, Mushrooms,
Poached Eggs, and Herb Oil, 73
Pumpkin Butter Pumpkin Spice Latté, 27
Pumpkin Caesar Salad with Sage Sourdough
Croutons, 123
Pumpkin Cardamom Donuts with Chai Glaze, 225
Pumpkin Deviled Eggs with Maple Pecan "Bacon,"
114
Pumpkin flesh, 13
Pumpkin Ginger Bread with Dark Chocolate and
Coconut, 78
Pumpkin Pie Granola with Pecans, 59
Pumpkin Pie Green Protein Smoothie, 43
Pumpkin seed butter, 251
Chocolate Pumpkin Seed Butter Cups, 211
Pumpkin Seed "Nut" Milk, 49
Pumpkin seed oil, 13
Delicata Squash and Arugula Salad with
Pumpkin Seed Oil Vinaigrette, 128
Savory Herbed Pumpkin Oatmeal with Soft-
Boiled Eggs and Pumpkin Seed Pesto, 56
Pumpkin Seed Oil Shortbread Jam Squares, 207
Pumpkin seed pesto
Savory Herbed Pumpkin Oatmeal with Soft-
Boiled Eggs and Pumpkin Seed Pesto, 56
Savory Yogurt with Roasted Pumpkin, Black
Quinoa, Pumpkin Seed Pesto, and Chili, 71

Pumpkin seeds, 13, 252
  Dulce de Leche Pumpkin Mousse, 237
  Lemony Roasted Brussels Sprouts and Pumpkin
    Seeds, 148
  Mini Classic Pumpkin Pies, 204
  Morning Glory Pumpkin Muffins, 81
  Pumpkin Seed "Nut" Milk, 49
  roasted, 252
  Savory Herbed Pumpkin Oatmeal with Soft-
    Boiled Eggs and Pumpkin Seed Pesto, 56
  Simple Roasted Pumpkin Soup with Smoky
    Roasted Pumpkin Seeds, 89
  Super-Seed Pumpkin Spice and Apple Muesli,
    60
  Toast with Pumpkin, Kale, Mushrooms,
    Poached Eggs, and Herb Oil, 73
Pumpkin seed sauce, 251
Pumpkin spice, 13, 247
  Chocolate Pumpkin Seed Butter Cups, 211
  Classic Pumpkin Pie, 203
  Classic Pumpkin Spice Latté, 24
  Cookies of Plenty with Chocolate, Pumpkin,
    Cranberries, and Pumpkin Seeds, 208
  Fudgy Pumpkin Coffee Brownies, 222
  Gingerbread Pumpkin and Hazelnut Shake, 39
  Gingerbread Pumpkin Cheesecake with Pecan
    Oat Crust, 213
  Gluten-Free Pumpkin Sour Cream Pancakes, 64
  Homemade Pumpkin Butter Poptarts, 221
  Honeyed Pumpkin Spice Masala Chai, 47
  Maple Pumpkin Spice Pumpkin Seeds, 252
  No-Knead Pumpkin Breakfast Braids, 77
  Pumpkin Butter Pumpkin Spice Latté, 27
  Pumpkin Pie Granola with Pecans, 59
  Pumpkin Pie Green Protein Smoothie, 43
  Pumpkin Spice Hot Chocolate, 32
  Pumpkin Spice Latté Base, 23
  Pumpkin Spice Rugelach with Chestnut Jam,
    218
  Pumpkin Spice Smoothie Bowl, 40
  Salted Caramel Pumpkin Spice Latté, 28
  Spiced Pumpkin Oatmeal with Baked Pears and
    Pecans, 55
  Sticky Toffee Pumpkin Spice Pecan Truffles, 217
  Super-Seed Pumpkin Spice and Apple Muesli,
    60

  Vegan Coconut, Vanilla Bean, and Pumpkin
    Panna Cotta, 234
Pumpkin Spice Hot Chocolate, 32
Pumpkin Spice Latté, 23
  base, 23
  Classic Pumpkin Spice Latté, 24
  Pumpkin Butter Pumpkin Spice Latté, 27
  Salted Caramel Pumpkin Spice Latté, 28
Pumpkin Spice London Fog, 35
Pumpkin Spice Rugelach with Chestnut Jam, 218
Pumpkin Spice Smoothie Bowl, 40
Pumpkin Spiked Latté with Orange Peel, 31
Pumpkin Veggie Burgers with Halloumi and
  Avocado, 171

Q
Quaker Pie Pumpkin, 8
Quinoa
  Black Quinoa with Heirloom Pumpkin,
    Chestnuts, and Mint, 135
  Cornucopia-Stuffed Pumpkin, 160
  Mellow Meyer Lemon Pumpkin Curry Bowls,
    177
  Savory Yogurt with Roasted Pumpkin, Black
    Quinoa, Pumpkin Seed Pesto, and Chili, 71

R
Raisins
  Morning Glory Pumpkin Muffins, 81
Rapini and Roasted Garlic Pumpkin Galette with
  Rosemary Spelt Crust, 174
Red Kuri, 8
Red peppers
  Shakshuka with Pumpkin and Peppers, 63
Red wine
  Heirloom Pumpkin Gnocchi with Oven-
    Roasted Tomato Sauce, 180
Rice
  Grain Bowls with Apple Cider Vinegar-Roasted
    Pumpkin and Kimchi, 164
  Vegetable Brown Rice Sushi with Ginger
    Pumpkin Dipping Sauce, 108
  Warm Wild Rice with Spinach, Pumpkin, and
    Grapes, 142
  Wild Rice and Oat Flourless Pumpkin Pancakes,
    67

Rice paper wrappers
  Halloumi Pumpkin Parcels with Pomegranate
    and Black Sesame, 103
  Poppy Seed Pumpkin and Mango Salad Rolls,
    111
Ricotta
  Lasagna with Pumpkin Orange Béchamel and
    Ricotta Parmesan Béchamel, 191
Roasted Garlic Pumpkin Hummus, 107
Roasted Jarrahdale Pumpkin and Onions with
  Lemony Whipped Feta, 132
Roasted pumpkin, 243
  Grain Bowls with Apple Cider Vinegar-Roasted
    Pumpkin and Kimchi, 164
  Whole Roasted Cinderella Pumpkin, 151
Roasted Pumpkin Seeds with Sweet & Savory
  Variations, 252
Roasted Pumpkin with Onions, Pomegranate and
  Yogurt, 136
Romaine
  Italian Pumpkin Holiday Salad with Gorgonzola
    and Cranberry Dressing, 127
  Pumpkin Caesar Salad with Sage Sourdough
    Croutons, 123
Rosemary
  Maple Roasted Pumpkin Crostini with Avocado,
    Feta, and Balsamic Glaze, 103
  Rapini and Roasted Garlic Pumpkin Galette
    with Rosemary Spelt Crust, 174
  Toast with Pumpkin, Kale, Mushrooms,
    Poached Eggs, and Herb Oil, 73
  Vegan Pumpkin, Onion, and Spinach Lasagna
    with White Bean Ricotta, 195

S
Saffron
  Brown Butter and Saffron Whole Wheat
    Pumpkin Custard Cake, 215
Sage
  Cornucopia-Stuffed Pumpkin, 160
  Pumpkin Caesar Salad with Sage Sourdough
    Croutons, 123
  Savory Herbed Pumpkin Oatmeal with Soft-
    Boiled Eggs and Pumpkin Seed Pesto, 56
  Simple Roasted Pumpkin Soup with Smoky
    Roasted Pumpkin Seeds, 89

Socca Pizza with Roasted Squash, Brussels
  Sprouts, and Lemon, 191
Wild Mushroom and Pumpkin Barley Pesto, 168
Salted Caramel Pumpkin Spice Latté, 28
Salted Honey Pumpkin Crème Brûlée, 233
Savory Herbed Pumpkin Oatmeal with Soft-Boiled
  Eggs and Pumpkin Seed Pesto, 56
Savory Yogurt with Roasted Pumpkin, Black
  Quinoa, Pumpkin Seed Pesto, and Chili, 71
Scones
  Sharp Cheddar, Pumpkin, and Pecan Scones, 82
Seed oil. See Pumpkin seed oil
Seeds. See Pumpkin seeds
Seminole, 8
Sesame seed
  Halloumi Pumpkin Parcels with Pomegranate
    and Black Sesame, 103
  Morning Glory Pumpkin Muffins, 81
  Pho with Pumpkin, Spelt Noodles, Mushrooms,
    and Tofu, 90
  Roasted Garlic Pumpkin Hummus, 107
  Vegetable Brown Rice Sushi with Ginger
    Pumpkin Dipping Sauce, 108
Shakshuka with Pumpkin and Peppers, 63
Shamrock, 11
Sharp Cheddar, Pumpkin, and Pecan Scones, 82
Silky Pumpkin Ginger Soup with Clementine and
  Vanilla, 96
Silky Pumpkin Pasta with Roasted Brussels Sprouts
  and Crispy Leaves, 183
Simple Roasted Pumpkin Soup with Smoky
  Roasted Pumpkin Seeds, 89
Skillet Pumpkin with Brown Butter, Honey, and
  Clementine, 139
Smoky Roasted Pumpkin Seeds, 252
Snacks, 99–117
Socca Pizza with Roasted Squash, Brussels Sprouts,
  and Lemon, 191
Soups, 85–96
Sour cream
  Gluten-Free Pumpkin Sour Cream Pancakes, 64
Soy milk
  Brown Butter and Saffron Whole Wheat
    Pumpkin Custard Cake, 215
  Pumpkin Cardamom Donuts with Chai Glaze,
    225

Spaghetti

Black Pasta with Roasted Pumpkin and Chili, 173

Pho with Pumpkin, Spelt Noodles, Mushrooms, and Tofu, 90

Silky Pumpkin Pasta with Roasted Brussels Sprouts and Crispy Leaves, 183

Thai Coconut Soup with Pumpkin, Noodles, and Lime, 95

Spelt Pie Crust, 244

Spelt Pumpkin Spice Gingerbread Forest Animal Cookies, 227–228

Spelt spaghetti

Pho with Pumpkin, Spelt Noodles, Mushrooms, and Tofu, 90

Spice. *See* Pumpkin spice

Spiced Pumpkin Oatmeal with Baked Pears and Pecans, 55

Spinach

Mellow Meyer Lemon Pumpkin Curry Bowls, 177

Pumpkin Pie Green Protein Smoothie, 43

Warm Wild Rice with Spinach, Pumpkin, and Grapes, 142

Sprouts

Avocado Toast with Pumpkin Butter and Sprouts, 68

Bean and Red Lentil Pumpkin Chili with Zucchini, 167

Squash

delicata

Delicata Squash and Arugula Salad with Pumpkin Seed Oil Vinaigrette, 128

Star anise

Pho with Pumpkin, Spelt Noodles, Mushrooms, and Tofu, 90

Sticky Toffee Pumpkin Spice Pecan Truffles, 217

Strawberry Crown, 8

Sugar/Pie, 8–11

Super-Seed Pumpkin Spice and Apple Muesli, 60

T

Tahini

Honeyed Pumpkin, Fig, and Tahini Bites, 113

Lettuce Cups with Orange, Cumin Seed Roasted Pumpkin and Tahini Yogurt Dressing, 124

Roasted Garlic Pumpkin Hummus, 107

Tamari

Firecracker Stir-Fried Pumpkin, Bok Choy, and Cashews, 188

Grain Bowls with Apple Cider Vinegar-Roasted Pumpkin and Kimchi, 164

Pho with Pumpkin, Spelt Noodles, Mushrooms, and Tofu, 90

Thai Coconut Soup with Pumpkin, Noodles, and Lime, 95

Vegetable Brown Rice Sushi with Ginger Pumpkin Dipping Sauce, 108

Tea

Honeyed Pumpkin Spice Masala Chai, 47

Pumpkin Spice London Fog, 35

Thai Coconut Soup with Pumpkin, Noodles, and Lime, 95

Thyme

Cornucopia-Stuffed Pumpkin, 160

Easy Lentil Soup with Greens and Pumpkin, 93

Mushrooms and Kale Over Pumpkin Polenta, 187

Roasted Jarrahdale Pumpkin and Onions with Lemony Whipped Feta, 132

Silky Pumpkin Pasta with Roasted Brussels Sprouts and Crispy Leaves, 183

Toast with Pumpkin, Kale, Mushrooms, Poached Eggs, and Herb Oil, 73

Vegan Pumpkin, Onion, and Spinach Lasagna with White Bean Ricotta, 195

Wild Mushroom and Pumpkin Barley Pesto, 168

Toast with Pumpkin, Kale, Mushrooms, Poached Eggs, and Herb Oil, 73

Tofu

Curried Pumpkin Tofu Calzones, 196

Grain Bowls with Apple Cider Vinegar-Roasted Pumpkin and Kimchi, 164

Pho with Pumpkin, Spelt Noodles, Mushrooms, and Tofu, 90

Tomatoes

Bean and Red Lentil Pumpkin Chili with Zucchini, 167

Heirloom Pumpkin Gnocchi with Oven-Roasted Tomato Sauce, 180

Tomato paste

Apple and Cheese Melts with Pumpkin Ketchup, 162

Tortillas
Huevos Rancheros with Smoky Pumpkin Sauce, 75
Triamble, 11
Turban, 11
Turk's Turban, 11
Turmeric
Mellow Meyer Lemon Pumpkin Curry Bowls, 177
Twice-Baked Mashed Pumpkin and Apples with Pecan Oat Crunch, 146

V
Vanilla Roasted Pumpkin Wedges, 145
Vegan Coconut, Vanilla Bean, and Pumpkin Panna Cotta, 234
Vegan Pumpkin, Onion, and Spinach Lasagna with White Bean Ricotta, 195
Vegan Pumpkin Eggnog, 44
Vegetable Brown Rice Sushi with Ginger Pumpkin Dipping Sauce, 108
Vegetable stock
Easy Lentil Soup with Greens and Pumpkin, 93
Millet Couscous with Roasted Parsnips, Pumpkin, and Mint, 140
Mushrooms and Kale Over Pumpkin Polenta, 187
Silky Pumpkin Ginger Soup with Clementine and Vanilla, 96
Simple Roasted Pumpkin Soup with Smoky Roasted Pumpkin Seeds, 89
Wild Mushroom and Pumpkin Barley Pesto, 168

W
Walnuts
Italian Pumpkin Holiday Salad with Gorgonzola and Cranberry Dressing, 127
Mini Classic Pumpkin Pies, 204
Roasted Jarrahdale Pumpkin and Onions with Lemony Whipped Feta, 132
Warm Wild Rice with Spinach, Pumpkin, and Grapes, 142
Whiskey
Pumpkin Spiked Latté with Orange Peel, 31
Whole Roasted Cinderella Pumpkin, 151
Wild Mushroom and Pumpkin Barley Pesto, 168

Wild Rice and Oat Flourless Pumpkin Pancakes, 67
Wine
Heirloom Pumpkin Gnocchi with Oven-Roasted Tomato Sauce, 180
Worcestershire sauce
Pumpkin Caesar Salad with Sage Sourdough Croutons, 123

X
Xantham gum
Cookies of Plenty with Chocolate, Pumpkin, Cranberries, and Pumpkin Seeds, 208

Y
Yogurt
Brown Butter and Saffron Whole Wheat Pumpkin Custard Cake, 215
Gingerbread Pumpkin and Hazelnut Shake, 39
Heirloom Pumpkin Gnocchi with Mint and Garlic, 179
Lettuce Cups with Orange, Cumin Seed Roasted Pumpkin and Tahini Yogurt Dressing, 124
Mini Classic Pumpkin Pies, 204
Pumpkin Pie Green Protein Smoothie, 43
Pumpkin Spice Smoothie Bowl, 40
Roasted Pumpkin with Onions, Pomegranate and Yogurt, 136
Savory Yogurt with Roasted Pumpkin, Black Quinoa, Pumpkin Seed Pesto, and Chili, 71
Yokohama, 11

Z
Zucchini
Bean and Red Lentil Pumpkin Chili with Zucchini, 167

CONVERSION CHARTS

METRIC AND IMPERIAL CONVERSIONS

(These conversions are rounded for convenience)

Ingredient	Cups/Tablespoons/ Teaspoons	Ounces	Grams/Milliliters
Butter	1 cup = 16 tablespoons = 2 sticks	8 ounces	230 grams
Cream cheese	1 tablespoon	0.5 ounce	14.5 grams
Cheese, shredded	1 cup	4 ounces	110 grams
Cornstarch	1 tablespoon	0.3 ounce	8 grams
Flour, all-purpose	1 cup/1 tablespoon	4.5 ounces/0.3 ounce	125 grams/8 grams
Flour, whole wheat	1 cup	4 ounces	120 grams
Fruit, dried	1 cup	4 ounces	120 grams
Fruits or veggies, chopped	1 cup	5 to 7 ounces	145 to 200 grams
Fruits or veggies, puréed	1 cup	8.5 ounces	245 grams
Honey, maple syrup, or corn syrup	1 tablespoon	.75 ounce	20 grams
Liquids: cream, milk, water, or juice	1 cup	8 fluid ounces	240 milliliters
Oats	1 cup	5.5 ounces	150 grams
Salt	1 teaspoon	0.2 ounce	6 grams
Spices: cinnamon, cloves, ginger, or nutmeg (ground)	1 teaspoon	0.2 ounce	5 milliliters
Sugar, brown, firmly packed	1 cup	7 ounces	200 grams
Sugar, white	1 cup/1 tablespoon	7 ounces/0.5 ounce	200 grams/12.5 grams
Vanilla extract	1 teaspoon	0.2 ounce	4 grams

OVEN TEMPERATURES

Fahrenheit	Celsius	Gas Mark
225°	110°	¼
250°	120°	½
275°	140°	1
300°	150°	2
325°	160°	3
350°	180°	4
375°	190°	5
400°	200°	6
425°	220°	7
450°	230°	8